The Complete Hunter™

VENISON COOKERY

THE HUNTING & FISHING LIBRARY®

COWLES
Creative Publishing, Inc.

President: Iain Macfarlane
Executive V.P.: William B. Jones
Group Director, Book Development: Zoe Graul

VENISON COOKERY

Executive Editor, Outdoor Products Group: Don Oster
Book Development Leader: Ellen C. Boeke
Managing Editor: Denise Bornhausen
Project Managers: Lori Holmberg, Tracy Stanley
Editor: Janice Cauley
Advising Editor: Teresa Marrone
Associate Creative Director: Brad Springer
Art Directors: Mark Jacobson, Linda Schloegel
Desktop Publishing Specialist: Laurie Kristensen
Home Economists: Elizabeth Emmons, Nancy Johnson, Karen Linden
Dietitian: Hill Nutrition Associates, Inc.
V.P. Photography and Production: Jim Bindas
Studio Services Manager: Marcia Chambers
Studio Services Coordinator: Cheryl Neisen
Lead Photographer: Rex Irmen
Photo Assistant: Greg Wallace
Food Stylists: Susan Brue, Bobbette Destiche, Elizabeth Emmons,
 Melinda Hutchison, Nancy Johnson
Contributors: Tom Carpenter, Alejandro Mendoza
Production Manager: Kim Gerber
Production Staff: Curt Ellering, Laura Hokkanen, Kay Wethern
Contributing Photographers: Kim Bailey, Dennis Becker,
 William Lindner, Chuck Nields, Rebecca Schmitt, Steven Smith

Printing: R. R. Donnelley & Sons Co.
00 99 98 97 / 5 4 3 2 1

Copyright © 1997 by Cowles Creative Publishing, Inc.
Formerly Cy DeCosse Incorporated
5900 Green Oak Drive
Minnetonka, Minnesota 55343
1-800-328-3895

Library of Congress Cataloging-in-Publication Data

Venison cookery.
    p. cm. -- (Hunting and fishing library)
    Includes index.
    ISBN 0-86573-068-7
    1. Cookery (Venison) I. Cowles Creative Publishing. II. Series.
TX751.V46 1997
641.6'91 -- dc21   97-8256

Other outdoor books available from the publisher:
The Art of Freshwater Fishing, Cleaning & Cooking Fish, Fishing With Live Bait, Largemouth Bass, Panfish, The Art of Hunting, Fishing With Artificial Lures, Walleye, Smallmouth Bass, Dressing & Cooking Wild Game, Freshwater Gamefish of North America, Trout, Secrets of the Fishing Pros, Fishing Rivers & Streams, Fishing Tips & Tricks, Fishing Natural Lakes, White-tailed Deer, Northern Pike & Muskie, America's Favorite Fish Recipes, Fishing Man-made Lakes, The Art of Fly Tying, America's Favorite Wild Game Recipes, Advanced Bass Fishing, Upland Game Birds, North American Game Animals, North American Game Birds, Advanced Whitetail Hunting, Understanding Whitetails, Fly-Fishing Equipment & Skills, Fly Fishing for Trout in Streams–Subsurface Techniques, Fly-Tying Techniques & Patterns, Fly Rod Gamefish–The Freshwater Species, Wild Turkey, Bowhunting Equipment & Skills, Muzzleloading, Duck Hunting

Contents

Introduction

The Complete Hunter™ is proud to bring you *Venison Cookery*, a collection of nearly 150 recipes featuring venison meat. These all-new recipes range from traditional meatloaves and hearty soups to spicy stir-fries and elegant stuffed tenderloins – a selection guaranteed to please a wide range of tastes. There's even a section with recipes that are easy to prepare in deer camp.

Every recipe was developed and tested in our own test kitchen by professional home economists, then tasted and critiqued by The Complete Hunter staff and friends, to ensure that you get the very best we have to offer. We tested the recipes with white-tailed deer, but we've included a handy substitution chart (page 7) so you can use other hoofed big-game animals in these recipes.

Since venison is usually a center-of-the-plate item, we've made main dishes our biggest section. This section features a large number of ground-venison recipes, since that is one of the most popular ways to process deer, along with delicious, new recipes for steaks, chops, roasts and tenderloins. Other sections in the book have soups, stews and chilies, and "small meals," which includes appetizers, sandwiches and salads. There is even a comprehensive section on sausages and smokehouse specialties, featuring step-by-step instructions for special processes like stuffing sausages and smoking jerky.

Nutritional Information

Each recipe includes nutrition information and exchanges for weight management. If a recipe has a range of servings, the data applies to the greater number of servings. If alternate ingredients are listed, the analysis applies to the first ingredient listed; optional ingredients are not included in the analysis.

In general, the number of servings in a recipe is based on 4 ounces of uncooked, boneless meat, which is the serving size recommended by the United States Department of Agriculture (USDA).

USDA figures for nutritional analysis of venison are limited, but we have used the best information available at this time. Since ground venison varies in its fat content, we've analyzed all ground-venison recipes using a ratio of 20% fat. Recipes that call for any type of venison sausage use nutritional analysis derived from sausage recipes in this book.

Icons

You'll find the following icons with recipes throughout this book to help you in meal planning.

FAST (45 minutes or less for preparation and cooking)

VERY FAST (30 minutes or less for preparation and cooking)

LOW-FAT (10 or fewer grams of fat per serving)

Gaminess

One of the most frequent comments made about wild venison is that it has a "gamey" flavor. Granted, wild venison is nothing like beef or even domestic venison, but its flavor is one that should be appreciated for its own qualities. Occasionally, venison does have a strong, or gamey, flavor. If it does, use it in recipes that are highly seasoned or call for the meat to be marinated. A simple preparation technique, such as roasting or panfrying, should be used when the meat has a more pleasant and mild flavor.

It may be helpful to understand the various causes for gamey flavor in venison. One possible explanation is that the animal was killed during the peak of rut (breeding season), when it was not relaxed or feeding normally. By the same token, a deer that was running hard before it was killed or one that was taken with a poor shot may have a gamey flavor due to the stress put on it.

An older animal can have a strong flavor and tough meat, too, although no hunter will pass up the opportunity to take a trophy deer simply because it may not taste good.

What the animal eats has an effect on how its meat tastes, too. "You are what you eat" means a big difference in flavor between the meat of a deer on a straight diet of pungent plants, such as sagebrush, and that of a deer with access to cornfields.

Finally, how the meat is cared for and processed has a huge impact on the quality of the final product. It is important to field-dress your deer immediately and cool the carcass as quickly as possible; then keep it clean and have it processed as soon as you can by a reputable meat processor. Package it tightly; then freeze it for future enjoyment.

Substitution Chart

Although there are differences in flavor, texture and fat content among the meats from the various hoofed big-game species, you can successfully substitute them for deer in a recipe, keeping in mind the tenderness of the specified cut and that of the substitute. The substitution chart below tells you the various big-game cuts you can substitute for the most common deer cuts. In addition, a column with suggested cooking methods helps you make the most of specific cuts.

DEER CUT	TENDERNESS	SUBSTITUTE	COOKING METHOD
Tenderloin (whole)	Very tender	Tenderloin portion from moose, elk or caribou Loin portion from caribou, deer or antelope	Oven roast, grill
Loin (portion)	Tender	Loin portion from moose, elk or caribou Tenderloin (whole) from moose, elk or caribou	Oven roast, broil, grill, panbroil, panfry
Loin steak	Tender	Loin steak from moose, elk or caribou Tenderloin from moose, elk, caribou, deer or antelope	Broil, grill, panbroil, panfry
Loin chop	Tender	Loin chop from any big-game animal	Broil, grill, panbroil, panfry
Rump roast	Intermediate tender	Rump roast from any big-game animal Deer sirloin tip Rolled, tied bottom round from deer or antelope Eye of round from moose, elk or caribou	Oven roast, grill, braise
Round steak	Intermediate tender	Round steak from any big-game animal Sirloin steak from any big-game animal Loin chop from moose, elk, caribou, deer or antelope	Broil, grill, panbroil, panfry, stir-fry (strips)
Boneless rolled shoulder roast	Less tender	Boneless rolled shoulder roast from any big-game animal Rolled rib roast from moose, elk or caribou Boneless chuck roast from moose, elk or caribou	Braise
Bone-in chuck roast	Less tender	Bone-in chuck roast from any big-game animal Blade pot roast from moose, elk or caribou	Braise

Main Dishes

← Sweet & Sour Meatballs ⚫FAST

MEATBALLS:

1 lb. lean ground venison, crumbled
1 egg, beaten
1/2 teaspoon ground ginger
1/2 teaspoon salt
1/4 teaspoon garlic powder
1/4 teaspoon freshly ground pepper

1 can (20 oz.) pineapple chunks, drained
   (reserve liquid)
1/4 cup white vinegar
3 tablespoons soy sauce
2 teaspoons packed brown sugar
1 teaspoon ground ginger
1 tablespoon plus 1 teaspoon cornstarch
2 medium carrots, cut into 1/4-inch slices (1 cup)
1 small onion, sliced
1 medium green pepper, seeded and cut into
   1/4-inch strips (1 cup)
6 cups hot cooked white rice

6 servings

In large mixing bowl, combine all meatball ingredients. Shape mixture into 30 meatballs, about 1 inch in diameter. Set aside. In 2-cup measure, combine reserved pineapple juice and enough water to equal 1 cup, the vinegar, soy sauce, brown sugar and 1 teaspoon ginger. Set aside. In small bowl, combine pineapple chunks and cornstarch. Set aside.

Spray 12-inch nonstick skillet with nonstick vegetable cooking spray. Heat skillet over medium heat. Add meatballs. Cook for 5 to 7 minutes, or until meatballs are browned, turning occasionally. Drain.

Add pineapple juice mixture, carrots and onion to skillet. Bring to a boil over medium-high heat. Cover. Reduce heat to medium-low. Simmer for 13 to 15 minutes, or until vegetables are tender, stirring occasionally. Add pineapple chunks to skillet, stirring until smooth. Stir in green pepper. Cook for 4 to 5 minutes, or until pepper is bright green, stirring frequently. Serve over hot cooked rice.

Per Serving: Calories: 529 • Protein: 22 g. • Carbohydrate: 81 g.
• Fat: 12 g. • Cholesterol: 98 mg. • Sodium: 752 mg.
Exchanges: 3 1/2 starch, 2 medium-fat meat, 2 vegetable, 1 fruit

Barbecued Porcupine Meatballs ⚫FAST ↑

MEATBALLS:

1 lb. lean ground venison, crumbled
1/2 cup instant white rice
1/4 cup finely chopped onion
1/2 teaspoon salt
1/4 teaspoon freshly ground pepper
1/8 teaspoon cayenne

SAUCE:

1 bottle (12 oz.) chili sauce
2/3 cup grape jelly
1/4 teaspoon garlic powder
1/4 teaspoon cayenne

4 servings

Heat oven to 400°F. In large mixing bowl, combine all meatball ingredients. Shape mixture into 16 meatballs, about 1 1/2 inches in diameter. Arrange meatballs in 8-inch square baking dish. Bake for 15 minutes. Drain.

Meanwhile, combine all sauce ingredients in 1-quart saucepan. Bring to a boil over medium-high heat. Cook for 3 to 4 minutes, or until jelly is melted, stirring constantly.

Pour heated sauce over drained meatballs. Bake for 10 to 12 minutes, or until sauce is hot and bubbly. Serve meatballs over mashed potatoes or hot cooked noodles, if desired.

TIP: This recipe can be made into an appetizer if meatballs are made smaller.

Per Serving: Calories: 542 • Protein: 25 g. • Carbohydrate: 68 g.
• Fat: 20 g. • Cholesterol: 98 mg. • Sodium: 1478 mg.
Exchanges: 3/4 starch, 3 medium-fat meat, 2 vegetable, 3/4 fat

Apple-Venison Meatballs 🍳 FAST

- 1 lb. lean ground venison, crumbled
- 1 large tart apple, peeled, cored and shredded
- 2 tablespoons dehydrated minced onion
- ½ teaspoon salt
  Freshly ground pepper to taste
- ⅓ cup seasoned dry bread crumbs*
- 1 cup dry red wine
- 1 can (8 oz.) tomato sauce
- 1 teaspoon sugar
- 1 teaspoon dried rosemary leaves, coarsely crushed
- 2 tablespoons olive oil

4 to 6 servings

In large mixing bowl, combine venison, apple, onion, salt and pepper. Shape mixture into 30 meatballs, about 1 inch in diameter. Roll balls in bread crumbs to coat. In 4-cup measure, combine wine, tomato sauce, sugar and rosemary. Set aside.

In 12-inch nonstick skillet, heat oil over medium heat. Add meatballs. Cook for 5 to 7 minutes, or until meatballs are browned, turning occasionally.

Pour wine mixture over meatballs. Reduce heat to medium-low. Cover and simmer for 10 minutes, turning meatballs over once.

Substitute fresh crumbs for dried. (See instructions following Cabbage Rolls with Raisin Sauce, page 16.) Season crumbs to taste with dried oregano leaves, dried basil leaves and pepper.

Per Serving: Calories: 322 • Protein: 16 g.
• Carbohydrate: 13 g. • Fat: 20 g.
• Cholesterol: 68 mg. • Sodium: 620 mg.
Exchanges: ½ starch, 2 medium-fat meat,
½ vegetable, ¼ fruit, 2 fat

Baked Chimichangas

Baking these chimichangas makes them more healthful and less messy than the traditional fried version, and they taste just as good.

1 lb. lean ground venison, crumbled
1 medium onion, chopped (1 cup)
1 clove garlic, minced
1 can (10 oz.) diced tomatoes with chilies
1/4 cup water
1/4 cup slivered almonds (optional)
1 tablespoon chili powder
1 teaspoon dried oregano leaves
1 teaspoon ground cumin
1/2 teaspoon salt
1/4 teaspoon ground cinnamon
6 flour tortillas (10-inch)
1 egg, beaten
2 tablespoons margarine or butter, melted

6 servings

Heat oven to 450°F. In 12-inch nonstick skillet, cook venison, onion and garlic over medium heat for 6 to 8 minutes, or until meat is no longer pink, stirring occasionally. Drain.

Return to heat. Add tomatoes, water, almonds, chili powder, oregano, cumin, salt and cinnamon to skillet. Bring to a simmer. Simmer for 8 to 10 minutes, or until liquid is nearly gone but mixture is still moist, stirring occasionally.

Spoon about 1/2 cup meat mixture onto center of 1 tortilla. Fold bottom third of tortilla over filling. Fold in sides. Brush top edge of tortilla with beaten egg. Fold down top of tortilla to seal. Repeat with remaining tortillas and meat mixture. Place chimichangas seam-side-down on baking sheet.

Brush tops of chimichangas with melted margarine. Bake for 12 to 15 minutes, or until tops are browned. Serve chimichangas with sour cream, shredded Cheddar cheese and salsa, if desired.

Per Serving: Calories: 406 • Protein: 21 g. • Carbohydrate: 36 g. • Fat: 19 g.
• Cholesterol: 98 mg. • Sodium: 735 mg.
Exchanges: 2 starch, 2 medium-fat meat, 1 vegetable, 2 fat

Classic Pasta Sauce

LOW-FAT

1 lb. lean ground venison, crumbled
1 medium onion, chopped (1 cup)
4 cloves garlic, minced
1 can (28 oz.) diced tomatoes, undrained
1 can (14½ oz.) tomato sauce
¼ cup tomato paste
1 tablespoon dried oregano leaves
2 teaspoons dried basil leaves
1 teaspoon sugar
1 bay leaf
¼ teaspoon red pepper flakes (optional)

Makes 7 cups

In 6-quart Dutch oven or stockpot, cook venison, onion and garlic over medium heat for 6 to 8 minutes, or until meat is no longer pink, stirring occasionally. Drain.

Stir in remaining ingredients. Bring to a boil over medium-high heat. Reduce heat to medium-low. Simmer for 30 to 45 minutes, or until flavors are blended and sauce is desired consistency, stirring occasionally. Remove and discard bay leaf.

Serve sauce over hot cooked pasta with shredded fresh Parmesan cheese, if desired.

Per ½ cup: Calories: 100 • Protein: 7 g.
• Carbohydrate: 7 g. • Fat: 5 g.
• Cholesterol: 27 mg. • Sodium: 321 mg.
Exchanges: ¾ medium-fat meat,
1½ vegetable, ¼ fat

Classic Mushroom-Wild Rice Casserole

This recipe is a good way to use up leftover rice. We call for wild rice here, but you can substitute any other rice or a blend of rices.

2 tablespoons vegetable oil
16 oz. fresh mushrooms, sliced (6 cups)
1 medium onion, chopped (1 cup)
½ cup sliced celery
4 cloves garlic, minced
1 lb. lean ground venison, crumbled
4 cups cooked wild rice

1 carton (16 oz.) low-fat sour cream
3 tablespoons all-purpose flour
1 teaspoon dried thyme leaves
1 teaspoon salt
½ teaspoon pepper
¼ teaspoon cayenne
½ cup sliced roasted red pepper*
⅓ cup slivered almonds

6 servings

Heat oven to 400°F. Spray 3-quart casserole with nonstick vegetable cooking spray. Set aside. In 12-inch nonstick skillet, heat oil over medium-high heat. Add mushrooms, onion, celery and garlic. Cook for 6 to 8 minutes, or until vegetables are tender, stirring frequently. Spoon vegetables into casserole. Set aside.

In same skillet, cook venison over medium-high heat for 5 to 7 minutes, or until meat is no longer pink, stirring frequently. Drain. Add meat and rice to casserole. In small bowl, combine sour cream, flour, thyme, salt, pepper and cayenne. Add sour cream mixture and red pepper to casserole. Stir to combine.

Sprinkle almonds evenly over top of meat mixture. Bake for 40 to 45 minutes, or until casserole is hot and bubbly.

Use roasted red peppers from a jar, or roast your own. To roast a pepper, place it under broiler with surface of pepper 3 to 4 inches from heat. Turn pepper frequently until skin is blackened and blistered. Seal pepper in plastic or paper bag, and let steam for 10 minutes to loosen skin. Peel pepper; proceed as directed.

Per Serving: Calories: 490 • Protein: 25 g. • Carbohydrate: 45 g. • Fat: 25 g.
• Cholesterol: 87 mg. • Sodium: 513 mg.
Exchanges: 2 starch, 2 medium-fat meat, 1½ vegetable, 3 fat

Calzones

DOUGH:

- 1 cup warm water (105° to 115°F)
- 1 tablespoon quick-rise active dry yeast
- 2 tablespoons olive oil
- 1 teaspoon salt
- 2½ to 3 cups all-purpose flour

FILLING:

- 1 lb. lean ground venison, crumbled
- 1 small onion, chopped (½ cup)
- 2 cloves garlic, minced
- 1¼ cups prepared pasta sauce
- 1 cup sliced fresh mushrooms
- 1 can (2¼ oz.) sliced black olives, drained
- 1 to 2 teaspoons Italian seasoning
- ½ teaspoon fennel seed, crushed
- ¼ teaspoon red pepper flakes (optional)
- 1½ cups shredded mozzarella cheese

- 1 egg, beaten

6 servings

In large mixing bowl, combine water and yeast. Let stand 5 minutes, or until bubbly. Stir in oil and salt. Add 2 cups flour; beat until smooth. Stir in enough of remaining flour until dough pulls away from side of bowl.

Turn dough out onto lightly floured surface. Knead for 5 to 10 minutes, or until smooth and elastic, adding flour as necessary to reduce stickiness. Place dough in medium mixing bowl that has been sprayed with nonstick vegetable cooking spray, turning dough to coat. Cover with plastic wrap. Let rise in warm place for 20 to 30 minutes, or until dough has doubled in size.

Meanwhile, combine venison, onion and garlic in 10-inch skillet. Cook over medium heat for 6 to 8 minutes, or until meat is no longer pink, stirring occasionally. Drain. Stir in pasta sauce, mushrooms, olives, Italian seasoning, fennel seed and red pepper flakes. Set filling aside.

Heat oven to 350°F. Punch down dough. Divide dough into 6 equal pieces. On lightly floured surface, roll dough into 7-inch circles. Spread ½ to ⅔ cup filling over half of 1 circle to within 1 inch of edge. Top with ¼ cup cheese. Fold other half of dough over filling; pinch edges to seal. Using a large spatula, transfer calzone to baking sheet that has been sprayed with nonstick vegetable cooking spray. Repeat with remaining dough circles, filling and cheese. Let calzones rest for 10 minutes.

Brush tops of calzones with beaten egg. Bake for 20 to 24 minutes, or until golden brown.

TIP: To reheat leftover calzones, place them on a baking sheet in a cold oven. Heat oven to 350°F; bake for 15 to 17 minutes, or until heated through.

Per Serving: Calories: 595 • Protein: 29 g. • Carbohydrate: 59 g. • Fat: 27 g. • Cholesterol: 120 mg. • Sodium: 872 mg.
Exchanges: 3 starch, 3 medium-fat meat, 2½ vegetable, 2 fat

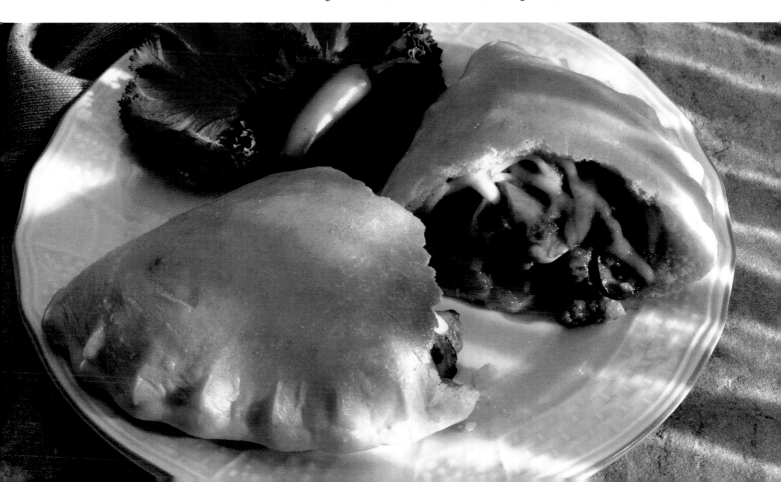

Cabbage Rolls with Raisin Sauce

12 cups water
6 large white cabbage leaves, thickest part of stem removed
1 lb. lean ground venison, crumbled
1 small onion, chopped (½ cup)
1 cup cooked wild or brown rice
1 cup fresh white bread crumbs*
½ cup chopped fresh mushrooms
2 eggs, beaten
¼ cup chopped tart apple
1 teaspoon salt
½ teaspoon pepper

SAUCE:

1 can (10½ oz.) beef consommé
1 can (8 oz.) tomato sauce
¾ cup golden raisins
1 tablespoon lemon juice
2 teaspoons paprika
1 teaspoon sugar
½ teaspoon white pepper

6 servings

Heat oven to 375°F. In 4-quart saucepan, bring water to a boil over high heat. Immerse cabbage leaves in water for 1 minute, or until color brightens. Remove leaves from water; drain on paper towels.

In 10-inch skillet, combine venison and onion. Cook over medium heat for 6 to 8 minutes, or until meat is no longer pink, stirring occasionally. Drain. Stir in rice, bread crumbs, mushrooms, eggs, apple, salt and pepper. Mix well.

Spoon approximately ⅔ cup venison mixture onto center of each cabbage leaf. Roll leaves up tightly, folding in sides. Place rolls seam-side-down in 8-inch square baking dish. Set aside.

In 4-cup measure, combine sauce ingredients. Pour sauce over rolls. Cover with foil. Bake for 30 to 40 minutes, or until sauce is bubbly and centers of rolls are hot.

To make fresh bread crumbs, remove crust from white bread. Process in blender or food processor until finely ground (1 slice = ½ cup crumbs).

Per Serving: Calories: 332 • Protein: 22 g. • Carbohydrate: 34 g. • Fat: 13 g. • Cholesterol: 134 mg. • Sodium: 1034 mg.
Exchanges: ¾ starch, 2 medium-fat meat, 1½ vegetable, 1 fruit, ½ fat

Venison Mexicali Pie →

1 lb. lean ground venison,
  crumbled
1 can (15 oz.) pinto beans,
  rinsed and drained
1 can (10 oz.) diced tomatoes
  with chilies, drained
1 teaspoon dried oregano leaves
1/2 teaspoon seasoned salt
1/4 teaspoon garlic powder
1/4 teaspoon pepper

BATTER:
1 1/2 cups skim milk
1 cup low-fat buttermilk baking
  mix
3 eggs, beaten
1 cup shredded Colby-Jack
  cheese

6 servings

Heat oven to 400°F. In 12-inch
skillet, cook venison over medium
heat for 6 to 8 minutes, or until no
longer pink, stirring occasionally.
Drain. Stir in beans, tomatoes,
oregano, salt, garlic powder and
pepper. Cook for 2 to 3 minutes,
or until heated through. Spray 10-
inch deep-dish pie plate with nonstick vegetable cooking spray.

Spread meat mixture in prepared
dish. In medium mixing bowl,
combine batter ingredients. Beat
with whisk for 1 minute. Pour batter evenly over meat mixture. Bake
for 25 minutes. Top evenly with
shredded cheese. Bake for 6 to 8
minutes, or until cheese is melted
and edges are golden brown. Let
stand for 5 minutes before cutting.

Per Serving: Calories: 407 • Protein: 28 g.
• Carbohydrate: 25 g. • Fat: 21 g.
• Cholesterol: 187 mg. • Sodium: 850 mg.
Exchanges: 1 1/4 starch, 3 medium-fat
meat, 1/2 skim milk, 1 fat

Cajun Meat Pasties

DOUGH:
4 1/3 cups all-purpose flour
1 teaspoon salt
1 cup vegetable shortening
3/4 cup cold water

1/2 lb. lean ground venison,
  crumbled
1 cup cubed red potatoes
  (1/4-inch cubes)
2/3 cup spicy vegetable juice
1/2 cup chopped carrot

1/2 cup frozen corn kernels,
  defrosted
1 small onion, finely chopped
  (1/2 cup)
1 tablespoon snipped fresh
  parsley
2 to 3 teaspoons Cajun
  seasoning
1/4 teaspoon salt
1/4 teaspoon pepper
1 egg white, beaten

8 servings

In large mixing bowl, combine flour and salt. Cut in shortening until mixture resembles coarse crumbs. Sprinkle with water, 1 tablespoon at a time,
while mixing with fork until particles are moistened and cling together.
Shape dough into ball. Wrap with plastic wrap. Chill 30 minutes.

Heat oven to 350°F. In 10-inch skillet, cook venison over medium heat
for 3 to 5 minutes, or until meat is no longer pink, stirring occasionally.
Remove from heat. Drain. Stir in remaining ingredients, except egg white.
Set filling aside.

Divide dough into 16 equal pieces. On lightly floured surface, roll 1 piece
into 6-inch circle. Place 3 heaping tablespoons filling on lower half of circle.
Fold top half of dough over filling. Press edges together with tines of fork.
Place pasty on ungreased baking sheet. Repeat with remaining dough and
filling. Brush tops of pasties with beaten egg white. Bake for 25 to 35
minutes, or until golden brown.

Per Serving: Calories: 571 • Protein: 14 g. • Carbohydrate: 60 g. • Fat: 30 g.
• Cholesterol: 23 mg. • Sodium: 689 mg.
Exchanges: 3 1/2 starch, 1/2 medium-fat meat, 1 1/2 vegetable, 5 1/2 fat

Stuffed Zucchini *LOW-FAT* ↑

3 medium zucchini (9 oz. each)
8 oz. lean ground venison, crumbled
1 cup chopped fresh mushrooms
2 cloves garlic, minced
¼ cup thinly sliced green onions
3 tablespoons julienned sun-dried tomatoes in marinade, drained, finely chopped
1 teaspoon dried oregano leaves
1 teaspoon dried basil leaves
¼ teaspoon salt
¼ teaspoon freshly ground pepper
2 teaspoons Worcestershire sauce
¼ cup shredded fresh Parmesan cheese or Cheddar cheese

6 servings

Heat oven to 375°F. Cut zucchini in half lengthwise. Scoop out pulp, leaving ¼-inch shells intact. (A grapefruit spoon makes it easy to scoop out pulp.) Coarsely chop pulp. Set shells and pulp aside.

In 12-inch nonstick skillet, cook venison over medium heat for 4 to 6 minutes, or until meat is no longer pink, stirring occasionally. Drain. Stir in reserved pulp, the mushrooms and garlic. Cook for 4 to 6 minutes, or until vegetables are tender-crisp, stirring occasionally. Stir in onions, tomatoes, oregano, basil, salt and pepper.

Brush insides of shells evenly with Worcestershire sauce. Spoon venison mixture evenly into shells. Arrange stuffed shells in 13 × 9-inch baking dish. Cover with foil. Bake for 25 to 30 minutes, or until shells are tender-crisp. Sprinkle evenly with cheese. Let stand for 5 minutes before serving.

Per Serving: Calories: 161 • Protein: 11 g. • Carbohydrate: 8 g. • Fat: 10 g. • Cholesterol: 34 mg. • Sodium: 195 mg.
Exchanges: 1 medium-fat meat, 1½ vegetable, 1 fat

Tamale Pie

1 lb. lean ground venison, crumbled
1 medium onion, chopped (1 cup)
1 medium green pepper, seeded and chopped (1 cup)
1 clove garlic, minced
1½ cups frozen corn kernels, defrosted
1 can (15 oz.) diced tomatoes with chilies, drained
2 tablespoons chili powder
½ teaspoon salt
¼ teaspoon pepper
1 cup shredded Cheddar cheese

BATTER:
2 cups water
¾ cup yellow cornmeal
3 tablespoons margarine or butter, melted

8 servings

Heat oven to 350°F. In 12-inch skillet, cook venison, onion, green pepper and garlic over medium heat for 6 to 8 minutes, or until meat is no longer pink, stirring occasionally. Drain.

Stir in corn, tomatoes, chili powder, salt and pepper. Spoon mixture into 13 × 9-inch baking dish that has been sprayed with nonstick vegetable cooking spray. Top evenly with cheese. Set aside.

In medium mixing bowl, combine batter ingredients. Pour batter evenly over meat mixture. Bake for 40 to 50 minutes, or until crust has formed and is golden brown.

Per Serving: Calories: 313 • Protein: 17 g. • Carbohydrate: 22 g. • Fat: 18 g. • Cholesterol: 62 mg. • Sodium: 533 mg.
Exchanges: 1 starch, 2 medium-fat meat, 1½ vegetable, 1½ fat

Moussaka

Moussaka is a traditional Greek dish commonly made with layered eggplants and ground lamb and topped with a Béchamel sauce. Venison's rich flavor is a perfect substitute for lamb.

2 medium eggplants (1 lb. each), cut into ½-inch slices

1 lb. lean ground venison, crumbled

1 medium onion, finely chopped (1 cup)

1 can (28 oz.) diced tomatoes, undrained

2 teaspoons dried oregano leaves

1 to 2 cloves garlic, minced

1 bay leaf

¼ teaspoon salt

¼ teaspoon freshly ground pepper

BÉCHAMEL SAUCE:

¼ cup butter or margarine

¼ cup all-purpose flour

2 cups 1% milk

¼ teaspoon salt

⅛ teaspoon white pepper

⅛ teaspoon ground nutmeg

½ cup shredded fresh Parmesan cheese, divided

8 servings

Per Serving: Calories: 271 • Protein: 16 g.
• Carbohydrate: 20 g. • Fat: 15 g.
• Cholesterol: 65 mg. • Sodium: 417 mg.
Exchanges: ¼ starch, 1½ medium-fat meat, 2½ vegetable, ¼ low-fat milk, 1¼ fat

Heat broiler. Spray large baking sheet with nonstick vegetable cooking spray. Arrange eggplant slices in single layer on prepared baking sheet. Place under broiler with surface of slices 3 to 4 inches from heat. Broil for 20 to 25 minutes, or until browned, turning slices over once and rearranging slices as necessary for even browning. Set aside.

Heat oven to 350°F. Adjust rack in oven to middle position. Spray 13 × 9-inch baking dish with nonstick vegetable cooking spray. Set aside.

In 12-inch nonstick skillet, cook venison and onion over medium heat for 6 to 8 minutes, or until meat is no longer pink, stirring occasionally. Drain. Stir in tomatoes, oregano, garlic, bay leaf, ¼ teaspoon salt and the ground pepper. Bring to a boil over medium heat. Simmer for 20 to 25 minutes, or until liquid is nearly gone, stirring occasionally. Remove and discard bay leaf. Set meat mixture aside.

Meanwhile, prepare sauce by melting butter in 2-quart saucepan over medium-low heat. Whisk in flour. Cook for 2 minutes, stirring constantly. Gradually whisk in milk. Add ¼ teaspoon salt, the white pepper and nutmeg. Increase heat to medium. Cook for 10 to 12 minutes, or until sauce is thickened, stirring constantly. Stir in ¼ cup Parmesan cheese until melted. Set sauce aside and keep warm.

Spread ½ of eggplant slices evenly in bottom of prepared dish. Top with half of meat mixture. Repeat layers. Pour sauce evenly over top. Sprinkle with remaining ¼ cup Parmesan cheese. Bake for 30 to 35 minutes, or until sauce is bubbly and top is light golden brown. Let stand for 5 minutes before cutting.

Shepherd's Pie

1 lb. lean ground venison, crumbled
1 medium zucchini, chopped (1½ cups)
⅓ cup sliced green onions
1 can (14½ oz.) cream-style corn
⅓ cup chopped red pepper
½ teaspoon dried thyme leaves
¼ teaspoon salt
¼ teaspoon pepper
2 tablespoons butter or margarine
3 cloves garlic, minced
3 cups mashed potatoes
½ cup shredded Cheddar cheese
Paprika

6 servings

Per Serving: Calories: 401 • Protein: 20 g.
• Carbohydrate: 32 g. • Fat: 22 g.
• Cholesterol: 85 mg. • Sodium: 727 mg.
Exchanges: 2 starch, 2¼ medium-fat meat, ¼ vegetable, 2 fat

Heat oven to 400°F. Spray 8-inch baking dish with non-stick vegetable cooking spray. Set aside. In 10-inch skillet, cook venison over medium heat for 6 to 8 minutes, or until meat is no longer pink, stirring occasionally. Drain.

Add zucchini and onions. Cook for 3 to 4 minutes, or until vegetables are tender, stirring occasionally. Remove from heat. Stir in corn, red pepper, thyme, salt and pepper. Spoon mixture into prepared baking dish. Set aside.

In 2-quart saucepan, melt butter over medium heat. Add garlic. Cook for 30 seconds, stirring constantly. Stir in potatoes until smooth. Stir in cheese. Spoon potato mixture over meat mixture, swirling potato topping decoratively. Sprinkle top with paprika.

Bake for 30 to 35 minutes, or until bubbly around edges. If desired, place under broiler with surface of potatoes 4 to 5 inches from heat for 2 to 3 minutes, or until potatoes are lightly browned.

TIP: To substitute instant potatoes for mashed potatoes, melt butter and cook garlic as directed above. Then add instant potatoes and water, and prepare as directed on package.

Spanikopita

Spanikopita is a favorite savory Greek pie made with a phyllo dough crust and a filling of spinach, onions, feta cheese, eggs and seasonings. Ground venison goes perfectly with the pie's full flavors.

½ lb. lean ground venison, crumbled
1 tablespoon olive oil
1 medium onion, finely chopped (1 cup)
2 pkgs. (10 oz. each) frozen chopped spinach, defrosted and well drained
8 oz. feta cheese with herbs, crumbled

4 eggs, slightly beaten
½ cup snipped fresh parsley
1 tablespoon dried dill weed
½ teaspoon pepper
½ cup butter, melted
12 sheets phyllo dough*

8 servings

Heat oven to 350°F. In 12-inch nonstick skillet, cook venison over medium heat for 3 to 5 minutes, or until meat is no longer pink, stirring occasionally. Drain. Set venison aside on paper-towel-lined plate. Wipe out skillet.

In same skillet, heat oil over medium heat. Add onion. Cook for 3 to 4 minutes, or until onion is tender, stirring frequently. In large mixing bowl, combine onion, venison, spinach, feta, eggs, parsley, dill weed and pepper. Mix well. Set aside.

Brush bottom and sides of 13 × 9-inch baking dish with melted butter. Remove phyllo from package and cut to fit dish. (Keep phyllo covered with plastic wrap to prevent it from drying out.) Place 1 sheet phyllo in bottom of dish. Brush with melted butter. Layer with a second sheet. Brush with butter. Continue layering and brushing with 4 more sheets. Spread spinach mixture evenly over phyllo. Layer and brush remaining 6 sheets as before.

Cut spanikopita into 8 squares all the way through to the bottom. Bake for 40 to 45 minutes, or until golden brown.

*Phyllo dough is a paper-thin pastry dough that is most commonly available frozen. It should be kept covered with plastic wrap and worked with quickly in order to keep it from drying out.

Per Serving: Calories: 405 • Protein: 18 g. • Carbohydrate: 21 g. • Fat: 28 g.
• Cholesterol: 181 mg. • Sodium: 573 mg.
Exchanges: 1 starch, 1¾ medium-fat meat, 1 vegetable, 3¾ fat

Stuffed Jumbo Shells

6 oz. uncooked jumbo pasta
   shells (18 shells)
1 lb. lean ground venison, crumbled
1 cup chopped fresh mushrooms
1 small onion, chopped (¹/₂ cup)
2 cloves garlic, minced
1 cup shredded part-skim
   mozzarella cheese
¹/₂ cup dry seasoned bread crumbs
1 egg, slightly beaten
1 teaspoon Italian seasoning
¹/₄ teaspoon ground nutmeg
1 jar (30 oz.) prepared pasta
   sauce (3 cups)
¹/₂ cup shredded fresh Parmesan
   cheese

4 to 6 servings

Heat oven to 350°F. Prepare shells as directed. Drain. Set aside.

Meanwhile, in 12-inch nonstick skillet, cook venison, mushrooms, onion and garlic over medium heat for 6 to 8 minutes, or until meat is no longer pink, stirring occasionally. Remove from heat. Drain. Stir in mozzarella, bread crumbs, egg, Italian seasoning and nutmeg.

Spoon half of pasta sauce in bottom of 12 × 8-inch baking dish. Stuff each shell with 2 tablespoons meat mixture. Arrange shells in dish. Pour remaining sauce over shells. Sprinkle shells evenly with Parmesan cheese. Cover with foil. Bake for 30 to 35 minutes, or until hot and bubbly.

Per Serving: Calories: 561 • Protein: 31 g. • Carbohydrate: 54 g. • Fat: 24 g.
• Cholesterol: 115 mg. • Sodium: 1256 mg.
Exchanges: 1¹/₂ starch, 2 medium-fat meat, 6 vegetable, 3 fat

Mock Chicken Fried Steak ● VERY FAST

1½ lbs. lean ground venison, crumbled
⅓ cup finely chopped onion
¾ teaspoon seasoned salt
1½ cups butter-flavored cracker crumbs (approximately 36 crackers)
1 egg, beaten
¼ cup skim milk
3 tablespoons vegetable oil, divided

6 servings

In large mixing bowl, combine venison, onion and salt. Shape mixture into six ½-inch-thick patties. Place crumbs in shallow dish. In second shallow dish, combine egg and milk.

Dip patties first in egg mixture, then dredge in crumbs to coat. Heat 1½ tablespoons oil in 12-inch nonstick skillet over medium heat. Cook 3 patties for 4 to 6 minutes, or until browned and meat is no longer pink inside, turning patties over once. Remove patties from skillet. Set aside and keep warm. Repeat with remaining oil and patties.

Per Serving: Calories: 451 • Protein: 24 g.
• Carbohydrate: 13 g. • Fat: 33 g.
• Cholesterol: 137 mg. • Sodium: 383 mg.
Exchanges: ¾ starch, 3 medium-fat meat, 3½ fat

Chili-Mac Skillet Meal ● VERY FAST

1 lb. lean ground venison, crumbled
1 medium onion, chopped (1 cup)
3 to 4 cloves garlic, minced
1 can (28 oz.) diced tomatoes, undrained
1 can (8 oz.) tomato sauce
1 teaspoon celery seed
1 teaspoon chili powder
½ teaspoon sugar
½ teaspoon salt
¼ teaspoon freshly ground pepper
1 cup (4 oz.) uncooked elbow macaroni

4 to 6 servings

In 12-inch nonstick skillet, combine venison, onion and garlic. Cook over medium heat for 6 to 8 minutes, or until meat is no longer pink, stirring occasionally. Drain.

Stir in remaining ingredients, except macaroni. Bring to a boil over medium-high heat. Stir in macaroni. Cover. Reduce heat to medium-low. Simmer for 15 to 20 minutes, or until macaroni is tender, stirring occasionally.

Per Serving: Calories: 281 • Protein: 19 g. • Carbohydrate: 26 g. • Fat: 11 g.
• Cholesterol: 63 mg. • Sodium: 665 mg.
Exchanges: 1 starch, 2 medium-fat meat, 2 vegetable

Potato-Venison Egg Casserole

1½ lbs. uncooked fresh venison sausage, crumbled (see page 109)
1 pkg. (2 lbs.) frozen Southern-style hash browns
4 cups shredded Colby-Jack cheese, divided
2 cups skim milk
6 eggs, slightly beaten
1 medium onion, finely chopped (1 cup)
½ teaspoon hot pepper sauce
½ teaspoon salt
  Salsa (optional)
  Sour cream (optional)

8 to 10 servings

In 12-inch nonstick skillet, cook sausage over medium heat for 6 to 8 minutes, or until meat is no longer pink. Drain.

In large mixing bowl, combine sausage, hash browns, 3 cups cheese, the milk, eggs, onion, hot pepper sauce and salt. Pour mixture into 13 × 9-inch baking dish that has been sprayed with nonstick vegetable cooking spray. Sprinkle evenly with remaining 1 cup cheese.

Cover with foil. Refrigerate several hours or overnight. Remove foil. Place casserole in oven. Heat oven to 350°F. Bake for 60 to 70 minutes, or until knife inserted in center comes out clean and top is browned. Let stand for 10 minutes before cutting. Garnish individual servings with salsa and sour cream.

Per Serving: Calories: 462 • Protein: 29 g. • Carbohydrate: 23 g. • Fat: 27 g. • Cholesterol: 225 mg. • Sodium: 741 mg. Exchanges: 1¼ starch, 4 medium-fat meat, 1½ fat

Venison Guisado ↑

Guisado is a Mexican staple. It literally translates to "cooked with seasonings," and basically is a fried meat dish with spicy seasonings. The mixture can be served wrapped in a flour tortilla with refried beans, cheese and salsa.

1 lb. lean ground venison, crumbled
2 medium onions, chopped (2 cups)
3 medium tomatoes, chopped (3 cups)
¼ cup water
1 to 3 jalapeño peppers, seeded and sliced

SPICES:
1½ teaspoons ground cumin
1 teaspoon chili powder
½ teaspoon garlic powder

½ teaspoon salt
½ teaspoon freshly ground pepper
¼ teaspoon cayenne
1 can (16 oz.) fat-free refried beans
8 flour tortillas (8-inch)
2 cups (8 oz.) shredded Cheddar cheese

GARNISHES (optional):
  Salsa
  Sour cream

8 servings

In 12-inch nonstick skillet, combine venison and onions. Cook over medium heat for 6 to 8 minutes, or until meat is no longer pink, stirring occasionally. Drain. Stir in tomatoes, water, jalapeños and spices. Bring to a boil. Simmer for 30 to 40 minutes, or until liquid cooks away but mixture is still moist, stirring occasionally.

In 1-quart saucepan, heat beans over medium-low heat, stirring occasionally. Warm tortillas as directed on package. Spoon ½ cup meat mixture and 2 heaping tablespoons beans across center of each tortilla. Sprinkle ¼ cup of cheese over each. Roll up tortilla, pinning shut with wooden pick.

If desired, microwave each rolled-up tortilla on High for 45 to 60 seconds, or until cheese is melted, rotating dish once. Serve tortillas topped with salsa and sour cream.

Per Serving: Calories: 425 • Protein: 25 g. • Carbohydrate: 36 g. • Fat: 20 g. • Cholesterol: 77 mg. • Sodium: 695 mg. Exchanges: 2 starch, 2½ medium-fat meat, 1 vegetable, 1½ fat

Herbed Meatloaf

MEATLOAF:
- 1 lb. lean ground venison, crumbled
- ½ lb. ground pork
- ¾ cup dry seasoned stuffing mix
- 1 small onion, finely chopped (½ cup)
- ⅓ cup chopped celery
- 1 egg, beaten
- 2 cloves garlic, minced
- ¾ teaspoon salt
- ½ teaspoon rubbed sage
- ½ teaspoon dried thyme leaves
- ¼ teaspoon pepper

SAUCE:
- 3 tablespoons finely chopped shallots
- 1 tablespoon butter or margarine
- 1 tablespoon all-purpose flour
- 1 cup ready-to-serve beef broth
- ¼ teaspoon dried thyme leaves
- ⅛ teaspoon pepper

6 to 8 servings

Heat oven to 375°F. Spray 9 × 5-inch loaf pan with nonstick vegetable cooking spray. In large mixing bowl, combine meatloaf ingredients. Press mixture into prepared pan.

Bake for 50 to 60 minutes, or until meat is firm and internal temperature reads 150°F. Let stand for 5 minutes before slicing.

Meanwhile, combine shallots and butter in 1-quart saucepan. Cook over medium heat for 2 to 3 minutes, or until shallots are tender, stirring frequently. Stir in flour. Gradually blend in broth, thyme and pepper. Cook for 2 to 3 minutes, or until gravy thickens and bubbles, stirring constantly. Serve meatloaf with gravy.

Per Serving: Calories: 286 • Protein: 18 g.
• Carbohydrate: 8 g. • Fat: 20 g.
• Cholesterol: 102 mg. • Sodium: 471 mg.
Exchanges: ½ starch, 2¼ medium-fat meat, 1¾ fat

Italian Meatloaf

- 1½ lbs. lean ground venison, crumbled
- 1½ cups onion and garlic-flavored croutons
- 1 can (14½ oz.) diced tomatoes with Italian seasonings, drained
- 1 egg, beaten
- 1 tablespoon dried parsley flakes
- 2 teaspoons Italian seasoning
- ¼ teaspoon crushed red pepper flakes (optional)
- ¼ teaspoon freshly ground pepper

6 to 8 servings

Heat oven to 375°F. In large mixing bowl, combine all ingredients. Shape mixture into an oval. Place in 9 × 5-inch loaf pan.

Bake for 1 hour to 1 hour 15 minutes, or until meat is firm and internal temperature reads 150°F. Let stand for 5 minutes before slicing.

Per Serving: Calories: 279 • Protein: 18 g. • Carbohydrate: 7 g. • Fat: 19 g.
• Cholesterol: 103 mg. • Sodium: 234 mg.
Exchanges: ¼ starch, 2¼ medium-fat meat, ½ vegetable, 1¾ fat

Meatloaf with Roasted Vegetables

4	slices white bread, crusts removed, cut into 1/4-inch cubes
1	egg
3	tablespoons Worcestershire sauce, divided
2	tablespoons skim milk
1	medium onion, chopped (1 cup)
1/4	cup finely chopped fresh parsley
1/4	cup catsup
1	tablespoon Dijon mustard
2	teaspoons garlic powder
1/2	teaspoon salt
1/2	teaspoon pepper
1 1/2	lbs. lean ground venison, crumbled
3	tablespoons barbecue sauce
2	cups beef or venison stock
1	large sweet potato, peeled, cut in half crosswise, then sliced lengthwise into 16 wedges
4	medium red potatoes, halved
2	large carrots, each cut into 6 pieces
1	medium onion, cut into 8 wedges

6 servings

Heat oven to 375°F. In large mixing bowl, combine bread, egg, 2 tablespoons Worcestershire sauce and the milk. Stir in chopped onion, parsley, catsup, mustard, garlic powder, salt and pepper. Add venison. Mix well. Shape mixture into 8 × 5-inch loaf. Place in center of 13 × 9-inch baking pan. Spread barbecue sauce evenly over meatloaf. Set aside.

In 2-cup measure, combine stock and remaining 1 tablespoon Worcestershire sauce. Pour into pan around meatloaf. Arrange vegetables in pan around meatloaf. Cover with foil.

Bake for 45 minutes. Uncover. Bake for 35 to 40 minutes longer, or until meat is firm and vegetables are tender. Transfer meatloaf to serving platter. Arrange vegetables around meatloaf. Strain pan juices through fine-mesh sieve. Spoon some juices over meatloaf and vegetables. Serve remaining juices on the side.

Per Serving: Calories: 558 • Protein: 29 g. • Carbohydrate: 53 g. • Fat: 25 g. • Cholesterol: 137 mg. • Sodium: 927 mg. Exchanges: 2 starch, 3 medium-fat meat, 1 vegetable, 2 fat

Classic Lasagna

1 lb. uncooked fresh venison
   sausage (see page 109),
   crumbled
1 medium onion, chopped (1 cup)
2 to 3 cloves garlic, minced
2 cans (15 oz. each) tomato sauce
1 can (14½ oz.) diced tomatoes,
   drained
2 tablespoons snipped fresh parsley
1 teaspoon dried basil leaves
1 pkg. (12 oz.) uncooked lasagna
   noodles (12 noodles)
3 cups shredded part-skim
   mozzarella cheese, divided
1 pkg. (15 oz.) part-skim ricotta
   cheese
½ cup shredded fresh Parmesan
   cheese, divided
1 egg
1 teaspoon dried oregano leaves

8 to 10 servings

In 12-inch skillet, combine sausage, onion and garlic. Cook over medium heat for 6 to 8 minutes, or until meat is no longer pink, stirring occasionally. Drain. Stir in tomato sauce, tomatoes, parsley and basil. Bring to a boil over medium-high heat. Reduce heat to medium-low. Simmer for 10 minutes to blend flavors and thicken slightly. Remove from heat. Set sauce aside.

Heat oven to 350°F. Meanwhile, prepare noodles according to package directions. Drain. In medium mixing bowl, combine 1 cup mozzarella, the ricotta, ¼ cup Parmesan cheese, the egg and oregano. Mix well.

Spread 1¼ cups sauce in bottom of 13 × 9-inch baking dish. Top evenly with 4 noodles, half of ricotta mixture, 1¼ cups sauce and ⅔ cup mozzarella. Starting with noodles, repeat preceding layers once. Top evenly with remaining noodles, sauce and mozzarella. Sprinkle evenly with remaining ¼ cup Parmesan cheese.

Cover with foil. Bake for 40 minutes. Remove foil. Bake for 15 to 20 minutes longer, or until edges are bubbly and cheese is golden brown. Let stand for 10 minutes before cutting.

Per Serving: Calories: 463 • Protein: 30 g. • Carbohydrate: 39 g. • Fat: 21 g.
• Cholesterol: 99 mg. • Sodium: 1135 mg.
Exchanges: 2 starch, 3 medium-fat meat, 1½ vegetable, 1 fat

Cassoulet

12 oz. spicy bratwurst-style venison sausage (see page 109), sliced
2 teaspoons olive oil
1 medium yellow summer squash or zucchini, sliced (1 cup)
1 small leek, chopped (1 cup)
1 cup sliced fresh mushrooms
1 medium carrot, chopped (1/2 cup)
1 clove garlic, minced
1 can (15½ oz.) pinto beans, rinsed and drained
1 can (15½ oz.) Great Northern beans, rinsed and drained
1 can (14½ oz.) diced tomatoes, undrained
1 teaspoon dried thyme leaves
1 teaspoon dried basil leaves
1 teaspoon freshly ground pepper
½ teaspoon salt
¼ cup unseasoned dry bread crumbs
1 tablespoon butter or margarine, melted

4 to 6 servings

Heat oven to 350°F. In 12-inch nonstick skillet, cook sausage over medium heat for 6 to 7 minutes, or until browned, stirring occasionally. Remove sausage from skillet and place on paper-towel-lined plate. Set aside. Wipe out skillet.

In same skillet, heat oil over medium heat. Add squash, leek, mushrooms, carrot and garlic. Cook for 4 to 5 minutes, or until vegetables are tender-crisp, stirring occasionally. Remove from heat. Stir in sausage, beans, tomatoes, thyme, basil, pepper and salt.

Spoon mixture into 2-quart casserole. Bake, uncovered, for 35 to 40 minutes, or until casserole is hot and bubbly. Remove from oven. Heat broiler. In small bowl, combine bread crumbs and melted butter. Sprinkle crumbs evenly over cassoulet. Broil with surface of cassoulet 4 to 5 inches from heat for 1½ to 2 minutes, or until crumbs are lightly browned.

TIP: A mild sausage or summer sausage may be substituted for a spicy sausage. If a spicy flavor is desired, add ¼ teaspoon red pepper flakes to cassoulet with other seasonings.

Per Serving: Calories: 328 • Protein: 19 g. • Carbohydrate: 27 g. • Fat: 16 g.
• Cholesterol: 51 mg. • Sodium: 781 mg.
Exchanges: 1½ starch, 1½ medium-fat meat, 1 vegetable, 1½ fat

Wild Rice & Fruit-stuffed Squash

2 medium acorn squash
   (1½ lbs. each)
3 tablespoons butter or
   margarine, melted
   Salt and pepper to taste
   Hot water
¾ lb. uncooked fresh venison
   sausage (see page 109),
   crumbled

1 cup cooked wild rice
½ cup dried cranberries
¼ cup sliced green onions
¼ cup golden raisins
½ teaspoon dried rosemary leaves
½ teaspoon salt
⅛ teaspoon white pepper

4 servings

Heat oven to 350°F. Cut squash in half lengthwise. Scoop out and discard seeds. Place squash halves cut-side-up in 13 × 9-inch baking dish. Brush evenly with melted butter. Sprinkle with salt and pepper to taste. Pour hot water in bottom of baking dish to ¼-inch depth. Cover tightly with foil. Bake for 45 to 50 minutes, or until squash is tender.

Meanwhile, in 12-inch nonstick skillet, cook sausage over medium heat for 4 to 6 minutes, or until meat is no longer pink, stirring occasionally. Drain. Stir in remaining ingredients. Cook for 3 to 4 minutes, or until filling is heated through, stirring frequently. Spoon filling evenly into squash halves. Serve immediately.

Per Serving: Calories: 474 • Protein: 20 g. • Carbohydrate: 55 g. • Fat: 21 g.
• Cholesterol: 94 mg. • Sodium: 408 mg.
Exchanges: 2¼ starch, 2¼ medium-fat meat, 1¼ fruit, 2 fat

← Cranberry Venison & Rice LOW-FAT

2 tablespoons vegetable oil,
   divided
2 lbs. venison top round, cut into
   1-inch cubes, divided
3 medium onions, each cut into
   8 wedges
2 cups beef or venison stock
1 cup dry red wine
2 tablespoons balsamic vinegar
3 cloves garlic, minced
1 teaspoon dried thyme leaves
1 teaspoon salt
½ teaspoon pepper
1 pkg. (12 oz.) fresh cranberries
½ cup packed brown sugar
½ cup all-purpose flour
½ cup water
8 cups hot cooked white rice
   Snipped fresh parsley
   (optional)

8 servings

In 6-quart Dutch oven, heat 1 tablespoon oil over medium-high heat. Add half of venison cubes. Cook for 4 to 6 minutes, or until meat is no longer pink, stirring frequently. Using slotted spoon, remove meat from pot. Set aside. Drain pot. Repeat with remaining oil and venison.

Return meat to pot. Stir in onions, stock, wine, vinegar, garlic, thyme, salt and pepper. Bring to a boil over high heat. Reduce heat to low. Cover. Simmer for 1 to 1½ hours, or until meat is tender, stirring occasionally.

In medium mixing bowl, combine cranberries, brown sugar, flour and water. Stir into meat mixture. Cook for 5 to 8 minutes, or until sauce is thickened, stirring frequently. Serve mixture over rice. Garnish with parsley.

Per Serving: Calories: 564 • Protein: 34 g.
• Carbohydrate: 88 g. • Fat: 7 g.
• Cholesterol: 96 mg. • Sodium: 526 mg.
Exchanges: 3¾ starch, 3 very lean meat, 1 vegetable, ¼ fruit, 1½ fat

Cuban Venison  FAST LOW-FAT →

SAUCE:

1 medium mango, peeled and
   cubed
1/2 cup pineapple juice
3 tablespoons packed brown
   sugar
3 tablespoons lime juice
2 tablespoons catsup
2 tablespoons red wine vinegar
1/2 teaspoon salt

1 tablespoon garlic-flavored oil
   or olive oil
3/4 lb. boneless venison top round,
   cut into 1-inch cubes
1/2 cup chopped red onion
1/2 cup coarsely chopped red or
   green pepper
2 cloves garlic, minced
3 cups cooked white rice
1/2 cup raisins
1/2 cup dry-roasted peanuts

6 servings

In blender or food processor, process mango until smooth. In 1-quart saucepan, combine processed mango and remaining sauce ingredients. Bring to a boil over high heat, stirring occasionally. Reduce heat to medium-low. Simmer for 10 to 12 minutes, or until slightly thickened, stirring frequently. Set sauce aside.

In 12-inch nonstick skillet, heat oil over medium-high heat. Add venison, onion, pepper and garlic. Cook for 6 to 8 minutes, or until meat is no longer pink. Stir in rice, raisins, peanuts and sauce. Cook for 3 to 5 minutes, or until heated through, stirring occasionally.

Per Serving: Calories: 403 • Protein: 20 g.
• Carbohydrate: 60 g. • Fat: 10 g.
• Cholesterol: 48 mg. • Sodium: 281 mg.
Exchanges: 1 3/4 starch, 1 1/2 very lean meat, 2 1/4 vegetable, 1 fruit, 2 fat

Curried Venison VERY FAST LOW-FAT

1 1/2 cups water
1/4 cup dry sherry
   Pinch saffron
1 cup uncooked Basmati rice,
   rinsed and drained
1 teaspoon olive oil
1 lb. boneless venison top
   round, cut into 1-inch cubes
1 cup coarsely chopped red and
   green pepper

1 medium onion, cut into thin
   wedges
3/4 cup beef or venison broth
1 tablespoon honey (optional)
1 tablespoon curry powder
1/2 teaspoon dried thyme leaves
1/2 teaspoon ground ginger
1/2 teaspoon ground cinnamon
1/2 teaspoon salt
1 bay leaf

4 servings

In 2-quart saucepan, combine water, sherry and saffron. Bring to a boil over high heat. Stir in rice. Cover. Reduce heat to low. Simmer for 15 to 17 minutes, or until water is absorbed.

Meanwhile, in 12-inch nonstick skillet, heat oil over medium heat. Add venison cubes. Cook for 3 to 5 minutes, or until meat is no longer pink, stirring occasionally. Stir in remaining ingredients. Bring to a boil. Simmer for 10 to 12 minutes, or until sauce is reduced and vegetables are tender, stirring occasionally. Remove and discard bay leaf. Serve curried venison over saffron rice.

Per Serving: Calories: 354 • Protein: 32 g. • Carbohydrate: 43 g. • Fat: 5 g.
• Cholesterol: 96 mg. • Sodium: 510 mg.
Exchanges: 2 starch, 3 very lean meat, 1 vegetable, 1 fat

Spicy Chinese Venison & Onions ⬤FAST LOW-FAT ↓

MARINADE:

1 tablespoon cornstarch mixed with 1 tablespoon water
1 tablespoon soy sauce
1 tablespoon sesame oil
1 tablespoon Szechuan sauce
1 lb. boneless venison round or flank steak, cut into 2 × 1 × 1/4-inch strips

1 tablespoon soy sauce
1 tablespoon dry sherry
1 tablespoon Szechuan sauce
2 teaspoons sugar
1 tablespoon sesame oil
1 large clove garlic, crushed
1 large bunch green onions, cut diagonally into 1 1/2-inch pieces (1 cup)

SAUCE:

1 tablespoon cornstarch mixed with 1 tablespoon water

4 servings

In medium mixing bowl, combine all marinade ingredients. Add venison strips and toss to coat. Cover with plastic wrap. Chill at least 30 minutes.

In 1-cup measure, combine all sauce ingredients. Set aside. Heat wok or 12-inch nonstick skillet over high heat. Add 1 tablespoon oil and swirl for 30 seconds. Add venison mixture and garlic. Cook for 2 to 3 minutes, or until meat is no longer pink, stirring constantly.

Add onions. Cook for 30 seconds, stirring constantly. Stir sauce mixture and add to wok. Cook until sauce is thickened and glossy, stirring constantly. Remove from heat. Remove and discard garlic. Serve mixture over hot cooked rice, if desired.

Per Serving: Calories: 248 • Protein: 27 g.
• Carbohydrate: 10 g. • Fat: 10 g.
• Cholesterol: 96 mg. • Sodium: 782 mg.
Exchanges: 3 very lean meat,
1/4 vegetable, 2 fat

Gingered Venison Stir-fry ⬤VERY FAST LOW-FAT ↑

1/4 cup orange juice
1 teaspoon cornstarch
1/2 teaspoon grated fresh lime peel
2 teaspoons vegetable oil
1 lb. boneless venison round or flank steak, cut into 3 × 1/2 × 1/4-inch strips
1 tablespoon grated fresh gingerroot

1 medium green pepper, seeded and cut into strips
1 medium red pepper, seeded and cut into strips
1/2 cup sliced green onions
1 tablespoon soy sauce
4 cups hot cooked white rice

4 servings

In 1-cup measure, combine juice, cornstarch and peel. Set aside. Heat wok or 12-inch nonstick skillet over medium-high heat. Add oil and swirl for 30 seconds.

Add venison and gingerroot. Cook for 3 to 4 minutes, or until meat is no longer pink, stirring constantly. Using slotted spoon, remove venison from wok. Set aside.

Add peppers and onions to wok. Cook for 2 to 3 minutes, or until vegetables are tender-crisp, stirring constantly. Return venison to wok. Stir juice mixture and add to wok. Cook until sauce is thickened and glossy, stirring constantly. Remove from heat. Stir in soy sauce. Serve over rice.

Per Serving: Calories: 448 • Protein: 32 g.
• Carbohydrate: 63 g. • Fat: 6 g.
• Cholesterol: 96 mg. • Sodium: 322 mg.
Exchanges: 3 1/2 starch, 3 very lean meat,
1/2 vegetable, 1 fat

Garlic Venison Stir-fry ● FAST ▪ LOW-FAT →

SAUCE:

1	cup ready-to-serve chicken broth	2	cups fresh broccoli flowerets
2	tablespoons hoisin sauce	1	medium red pepper, seeded and cut into 1/2-inch chunks (1 1/2 cups)
1	tablespoon Szechuan sauce		
1	tablespoon cornstarch	4	oz. fresh snow pea pods, trimmed (1 1/2 cups)
1	tablespoon sesame seed		
1 1/2	teaspoons hot chili sauce	1	medium red onion, sliced
1	teaspoon sugar	1	cup sliced fresh mushrooms
1/2	teaspoon ground ginger	1	cup baby carrots
1	tablespoon garlic-flavored oil or sesame oil	1/2	cup bean sprouts
		4	to 6 cloves garlic, minced
1	lb. boneless venison top round, cut into 1-inch cubes		

6 servings

In 1-cup measure, combine sauce ingredients. Set aside. Heat wok or 12-inch nonstick skillet over medium-high heat. Add oil and swirl for 30 seconds. Add venison. Cook for 3 to 5 minutes, or until meat is no longer pink, stirring constantly. Stir in remaining ingredients, except rice. Stir sauce mixture and add to wok.

Bring to a boil, stirring occasionally. Reduce heat to medium-low. Simmer for 6 to 8 minutes, or until vegetables are tender-crisp, stirring occasionally. Serve over hot cooked rice, if desired.

Per Serving: Calories: 209 • Protein: 22 g. • Carbohydrate: 18 g.
• Fat: 6 g. • Cholesterol: 64 mg. • Sodium: 411 mg.
Exchanges: 2 very lean meat, 3 1/2 vegetable, 1 fat

STIR-FRY TIP: Stir-fry recipes cook up very quickly, so it is best to prepare all the ingredients and have them in bowls next to the stove when you are ready to begin cooking. The rice should be prepared ahead of everything, so it is ready when the stir-fry is.

Venison Bourguignonne ▪ LOW-FAT

 4 slices bacon, cut into 1-inch pieces
1½ lbs. venison top or bottom round, cut
      into ¾-inch cubes
 ¼ cup all-purpose flour
 2 teaspoons vegetable oil
 1 can (10½ oz.) beef consommé
 ¾ cup burgundy wine or other
      full-flavored dry red wine
 ½ cup water
 1 teaspoon salt
 ¼ teaspoon pepper
 1 bay leaf
 1 pkg. (16 oz.) frozen potato, carrot
      and pearl onion vegetable mix
 8 oz. small fresh mushrooms*
 ½ cup snipped fresh parsley
 6 to 8 cups hot cooked egg
      noodles

6 to 8 servings

In 6-quart Dutch oven, cook
bacon over medium-high
heat for 3 to 5 minutes, or
until browned, stirring frequently. Remove bacon
from pan. Set aside. Wipe
out pan with paper towels.

Dredge venison cubes in
flour to coat. In same Dutch
oven, heat oil over medium-
high heat. Add venison.
Cook for 5 to 7 minutes, or
until meat is browned, stirring frequently.

Stir in bacon, consommé, wine,
water, salt, pepper and bay leaf.
Bring to a boil. Reduce heat to
low. Simmer for 1½ to 2 hours,
or until meat is tender, stirring
occasionally. Stir in vegetable mix,
mushrooms and parsley. Bring to a
boil over medium-high heat. Reduce
heat to medium-low. Simmer for 20 to
30 minutes, or until vegetables are tender,
stirring occasionally. Remove and discard
bay leaf. Serve over noodles.

*Cut large mushrooms in halves or quarters
to equal size of whole mushrooms.

Per Serving: Calories: 403 • Protein: 31 g.
• Carbohydrate: 52 g. • Fat: 7 g.
• Cholesterol: 128 mg. • Sodium: 664 mg.
Exchanges: 2¾ starch, 2½ very lean meat,
1½ vegetable, 1½ fat

Oriental Venison, Noodle & Vegetable Stir-fry LOW-FAT

1 pkg. (9 oz.) Japanese curly noodles
1 lb. venison top or bottom round, cut into 2 × 1 × 1/8-inch strips
1 teaspoon sesame oil
1 teaspoon grated fresh gingerroot
1 pkg. (16 oz.) frozen stir-fry vegetable mix (sugar snap peas, carrots and mushrooms)
1/2 cup prepared stir-fry sauce*
1/4 cup water

4 to 6 servings

Prepare noodles as directed on package. Set aside and keep warm. Heat 12-inch nonstick skillet or wok over medium-high heat. Spray with nonstick vegetable cooking spray. Add meat. Cook for 4 to 6 minutes, or until meat is no longer pink, stirring frequently. Using slotted spoon, remove meat from skillet. Set aside and keep warm. Wipe out skillet with paper towels.

In same skillet, heat oil over medium-high heat. Add gingerroot. Cook for 30 seconds, stirring constantly. Add vegetable mix. Cook for 4 to 6 minutes, or until vegetables are tender-crisp, stirring frequently. Stir in venison, noodles, stir-fry sauce and water. Cook for 3 to 5 minutes, or until liquid is hot and bubbly, stirring constantly.

*Use your favorite prepared sauce–either spicy or mild.

TIP: It is easier to cut venison into very thin strips if it is partially frozen.

Per Serving: Calories: 301 • Protein: 26 g.
• Carbohydrate: 46 g. • Fat: 3 g.
• Cholesterol: 64 mg. • Sodium: 876 mg.
Exchanges: 2 starch, 2 very lean meat, 3 vegetable, 1/2 fat

← Finger Steaks ● VERY FAST

BATTER:
⅓ cup Dijon mustard
3 tablespoons water
2 teaspoons Worcestershire sauce
⅛ teaspoon cayenne

1 cup unseasoned dry bread crumbs
1 lb. boneless venison bottom round, cut into
    4 × 1 × ½-inch strips
¼ cup vegetable oil, divided
1 cup cocktail sauce

4 servings

In small mixing bowl, combine all batter ingredients. Place in shallow dish. Place bread crumbs in second shallow dish. Dip venison strips first in batter to coat lightly, then dredge in bread crumbs to coat.

In 12-inch nonstick skillet, heat 2 tablespoons oil over medium-high heat. Add half of strips. Cook for 4 to 5 minutes, or until golden brown, turning strips over once. Remove strips from skillet. Set aside on paper-towel-lined plate and keep warm. Repeat with remaining 2 tablespoons oil and half of strips. Serve finger steaks with cocktail sauce.

Per Serving: Calories: 496 • Protein: 30 g. • Carbohydrate: 45 g. • Fat: 18 g. • Cholesterol: 96 mg. • Sodium: 1564 mg.
Exchanges: 1½ starch, 3 very lean meat, 2 vegetable, 3½ fat

Venison in Mushroom-Wine Sauce

2 tablespoons butter or margarine
1 small onion, chopped (½ cup)
½ cup chopped carrot
¼ cup plus 3 tablespoons
    all-purpose flour, divided
1½ cups beef or venison stock
2 tablespoons tomato paste
½ teaspoon salt
⅛ to ¼ teaspoon white pepper
1 lb. boneless venison top round,
    cut into 1-inch cubes
1 tablespoon vegetable oil
8 oz. fresh mushrooms,
    quartered
½ cup Madeira wine
½ cup low-fat sour cream
6 cups hot cooked egg noodles
    or rice
    Snipped fresh parsley

6 servings

In 2-quart saucepan, melt butter over medium-high heat. Add onion and carrot. Cook for 3 to 4 minutes, or until vegetables are tender, stirring frequently. Stir in 3 tablespoons flour. Cook for 1 minute, stirring constantly.

Gradually blend in stock. Stir in tomato paste, salt and pepper. Bring to a boil. Reduce heat to medium-low. Simmer for 1 to 2 minutes, or until sauce thickens and bubbles, stirring frequently. Set sauce aside.

Place remaining ¼ cup flour in large plastic food-storage bag. Add venison pieces, secure bag and shake to coat. In 12-inch nonstick skillet, heat oil over medium-high heat. Add venison. Cook for 4 to 6 minutes, or until meat is browned, stirring occasionally.

Add mushrooms, wine, sour cream and sauce. Reduce heat to medium-low. Cover and cook for 10 to 14 minutes, or until mushrooms are tender, stirring occasionally. Serve mixture over noodles. Sprinkle with parsley.

Per Serving: Calories: 473 • Protein: 28 g. • Carbohydrate: 57 g. • Fat: 12 g. • Cholesterol: 134 mg. • Sodium: 546 mg.
Exchanges: 3½ starch, 2 very lean meat, 1 vegetable, 2½ fat

Black Bean & Rice Casserole

1 pkg. (6 oz.) Spanish rice mix
2 teaspoons olive oil
1 lb. boneless venison top round, chopped*
1 can (15 oz.) black beans, rinsed and drained
1 can (14½ oz.) diced tomatoes with chilies, undrained
½ cup sliced green onions
2 teaspoons chili powder
1 teaspoon ground cumin
⅛ teaspoon cayenne (optional)
½ cup (2 oz.) shredded Colby-Jack cheese (optional)
Sour cream for garnish (optional)

6 servings

Heat oven to 375°F. Prepare rice as directed on package. Meanwhile, in 12-inch nonstick skillet, heat oil over medium heat. Add venison. Cook for 3 to 5 minutes, or until meat is no longer pink, stirring occasionally. Remove from heat. Drain.

Stir in remaining ingredients, except cheese and sour cream. Mix well. Spoon mixture into 2-quart casserole. Sprinkle evenly with cheese. Bake, uncovered, for 25 to 30 minutes, or until casserole is hot and bubbly around edges. Garnish with sour cream.

TIP: Casserole can also be served as a filling for flour tortillas.

Per Serving: Calories: 260 • Protein: 23 g. • Carbohydrate: 32 g. • Fat: 4 g.
• Cholesterol: 64 mg. • Sodium: 812 mg.
Exchanges: 1½ starch, 2 very lean meat, 2 vegetable, ¾ fat

*How to Chop Venison

CUT meat across grain into thin strips. Cut strips lengthwise into smaller strips.

CHOP strips crosswise into small pieces.

Oriental Venison Kabobs ⏱ FAST ⬤ LOW-FAT

SAUCE:

½ cup red plum jam

3 tablespoons hoisin sauce

½ teaspoon hot chili sauce with garlic

¼ teaspoon garlic powder

2 lbs. boneless venison sirloin steaks, cut into 1-inch cubes

20 fresh whole mushrooms (8 to 10 oz.)

8 green onions, cut into twenty 1½-inch pieces

2 medium red peppers, cut into twenty 1-inch pieces

1 yellow, orange or green pepper, seeded and cut into ten 1-inch pieces

10 skewers (10 or 12-inch)

10 kabobs

In 1-quart saucepan, combine all sauce ingredients. Cook over medium heat for 3 to 4 minutes, or until bubbly, stirring frequently. Reserve half of sauce for basting and half for serving.

Assemble kabobs by threading meat and vegetables evenly on skewers. Prepare grill for medium direct heat. Spray cooking grid with nonstick vegetable cooking spray. Grill kabobs for 6 to 8 minutes, or until desired doneness, turning kabobs and basting with sauce once or twice. Serve kabobs with reserved sauce.

Per Kabob: Calories: 178 • Protein: 22 g.
• Carbohydrate: 17 g. • Fat: 2 g.
• Cholesterol: 77 mg. • Sodium: 152 mg.
Exchanges: 2½ very lean meat,
2 vegetable, ½ fat

Kabobs with Whiskey-Pepper Sauce

> 4 boneless venison loin steaks (4 oz. each), cut
>   into 4 × 1/2 × 1/4-inch strips
> 1 medium yellow summer squash, cut into
>   1/2-inch rounds (2 cups)
> 1/2 medium green or red pepper, cut into 16 chunks
> 1 small onion, cut into 8 wedges
> 4 skewers (12-inch)

SAUCE:

> 1 tablespoon butter
> 3 tablespoons finely chopped shallots or green
>   onions
> 1 1/2 cups beef or venison stock
> 1/2 cup dry white wine
> 1/4 cup plus 2 tablespoons sour-mash whiskey,
>   divided
> 1 tablespoon coarsely ground pepper
> 1/4 cup heavy whipping cream
> 1/2 teaspoon salt

4 servings

Thread venison strips, accordion-style, evenly with squash, green or red pepper and onion onto skewers. Refrigerate until ready to cook.

For sauce, melt butter in 2-quart saucepan over medium heat. Add shallots. Cook for 2 to 3 minutes, or until golden brown, stirring frequently. Stir in stock, wine, 1/4 cup whiskey and the ground pepper. Bring to a boil over medium-high heat. Cook for 10 to 15 minutes, or until sauce is reduced by half, stirring occasionally. Stir in cream. Continue cooking for 8 to 10 minutes, or until sauce reduces to 1 cup, stirring frequently. Remove from heat. Stir in remaining 2 tablespoons whiskey and the salt. Set aside and keep warm.

Heat broiler. Spray rack in broiler pan with nonstick vegetable cooking spray. Arrange kabobs on rack. Spray kabobs with nonstick vegetable cooking spray, if desired. Broil kabobs 4 to 5 inches from heat for 10 to 12 minutes, or until meat is no longer pink and vegetables are tender-crisp, turning kabobs occasionally. Serve kabobs with sauce.

TIP: Sauce is excellent served with steaks or roasts.

Per Serving: Calories: 269 • Protein: 28 g. • Carbohydrate: 8 g.
• Fat: 12 g. • Cholesterol: 123 mg. • Sodium: 667 mg.
Exchanges: 3 very lean meat, 1 vegetable, 2 1/4 fat

Mexican Roll-ups

1 lb. boneless venison round
    steaks, cut into 2 × 1 × ¼-
    inch strips
3 cloves garlic, minced
2 cups water
1 large onion, sliced
1 pkg. (1.5 oz.) enchilada
    sauce mix
1 teaspoon chili powder
⅛ teaspoon black pepper
⅛ teaspoon cayenne (optional)
10 flour tortillas (8-inch)
1¾ cups shredded Monterey Jack
    cheese, divided

5 servings

Heat 12-inch nonstick skillet over medium-high heat. Spray with nonstick vegetable cooking spray. Add venison and garlic. Cook for 4 to 6 minutes, or until meat is no longer pink, stirring frequently. Stir in water, onion, sauce mix, chili powder and peppers. Cover. Reduce heat to low. Simmer for 1 to 1½ hours, or until meat is tender, stirring occasionally.

Heat oven to 350°F. Spray 13 × 9-inch baking dish with nonstick vegetable cooking spray. Using slotted spoon, spoon approximately ¼ cup meat mixture into center of tortilla. Sprinkle with 1 tablespoon cheese. Roll up tortilla and place seam-side-down in baking dish. Repeat with remaining meat mixture, tortillas and 9 tablespoons cheese.

Spoon sauce over roll-ups. Cover dish with foil. Bake for 30 to 40 minutes, or until hot and bubbly. Top with remaining cheese. Let stand for 5 minutes. Garnish with chopped tomato, sliced green onions and sour cream, if desired.

Per Serving: Calories: 533 • Protein: 37 g. • Carbohydrate: 49 g. • Fat: 20 g. • Cholesterol: 119 mg. • Sodium: 1054 mg. Exchanges: 3 starch, 4 very lean meat, ¾ vegetable, 4 fat

Venison Paprikash ↑

¼ cup all-purpose flour
¼ cup sweet Hungarian paprika,
    divided
1 teaspoon dried marjoram
    leaves
1 teaspoon salt
¼ teaspoon pepper
1½ lbs. venison boneless sirloin
    tip, cut into 1-inch pieces
3 tablespoons olive oil

2 tablespoons margarine or
    butter
1 medium onion, chopped
    (1 cup)
2 cloves garlic, minced
½ cup dry red wine
½ cup beef or venison stock
½ cup orange juice
¼ cup sour cream
6 cups hot cooked egg noodles

6 servings

In large plastic food storage bag, combine flour, 1 tablespoon paprika, the marjoram, salt and pepper. Add venison pieces, seal bag and shake to coat. In 12-inch nonstick skillet, heat oil and margarine over medium heat. Add venison pieces, onion and garlic. Cook for 5 to 7 minutes, or until meat is browned, stirring frequently.

Stir in remaining 3 tablespoons paprika, the wine and stock. Bring to a boil. Reduce heat to medium-low. Simmer for 20 to 30 minutes, or until sauce is thickened, stirring occasionally. Increase heat to medium. Stir in juice. Simmer for 8 to 10 minutes, or until sauce is thickened, stirring frequently.

Remove from heat. Stir in sour cream until blended. Serve paprikash over noodles.

Per Serving: Calories: 520 • Protein: 36 g. • Carbohydrate: 52 g. • Fat: 18 g. • Cholesterol: 153 mg. • Sodium: 558 mg. Exchanges: 3 starch, 3½ medium-fat meat

Rum-spiced Venison Chops

1 tablespoon olive oil
1 medium onion, finely chopped (1 cup)
2 jalapeño peppers or other hot chili peppers, seeded and finely chopped
4 cloves garlic, minced
1/2 teaspoon dried thyme leaves
1/2 teaspoon ground cinnamon
1/8 teaspoon ground nutmeg
1/8 teaspoon ground cloves
1 bay leaf
1/4 cup dark rum
2 tablespoons fresh lime juice
1/4 teaspoon salt
4 bone-in venison loin chops (6 oz. each), 1/2 to 3/4 inch thick

4 servings

In 10-inch nonstick skillet, heat oil over medium heat. Add onion, jalapeños, garlic, thyme, cinnamon, nutmeg, cloves and bay leaf. Cook for 8 to 10 minutes, or until mixture is deep golden brown, stirring frequently.

Increase heat to medium-high. Stir in rum, juice and salt. Cook for 1 1/2 to 2 1/2 minutes, or until most liquid has boiled away. Remove from heat. Remove and discard bay leaf. Cool marinade completely.

Place chops in shallow dish. Spread half of marinade over chops. Turn chops over and spread with remaining marinade. Cover with plastic wrap. Chill 4 hours.

Prepare grill for medium direct heat. Spray cooking grid with nonstick vegetable cooking spray. Do not remove marinade from meat. Grill chops, covered, for 10 to 12 minutes, or until desired doneness, turning chops over once.

Per Serving: Calories: 192 • Protein: 27 g. • Carbohydrate: 6 g. • Fat: 6 g.
• Cholesterol: 95 mg. • Sodium: 184 mg.
Exchanges: 3 very lean meat, 1 1/4 vegetable, 1 1/4 fat

Pesto Venison Chops ↑

4 bone-in venison loin chops
  (6 oz. each), ½ inch thick
¼ cup prepared pesto
4 thin tomato slices
4 slices (3 oz. each) Provolone
  cheese
  Fresh basil sprigs (optional)

4 servings

Heat broiler. Spray rack in broiler pan with nonstick vegetable cooking spray. Arrange chops on rack. Broil 4 to 5 inches from heat for 3 to 5 minutes, or until meat is no longer pink, turning chops over once.

Spread pesto evenly over chops. Broil for 2 to 3 minutes, or until pesto starts to brown. Top each chop with 1 slice tomato and 1 slice cheese. Broil for 1 to 2 minutes, or until cheese is melted and lightly browned. Garnish with fresh basil sprig.

Per Serving: Calories: 513 • Protein: 49 g.
• Carbohydrate: 4 g. • Fat: 33 g.
• Cholesterol: 156 mg. • Sodium: 902 mg.
Exchanges: 6 medium-fat meat,
¾ vegetable, ½ fat

Blackened Venison Chops ⬤ VERY FAST ⬤ LOW-FAT

SPICE MIX:
2 tablespoons black and red
  pepper blend*
2 tablespoons paprika
1 tablespoon garlic powder
1 tablespoon onion powder
2 teaspoons salt

2 tablespoons butter or margarine,
  melted
4 bone-in venison loin chops
  (6 oz. each), ½ inch thick

4 servings

In shallow dish, combine all spice mix ingredients. Set aside. Place melted butter in second shallow dish.

Dip chops first in melted butter, then dredge in spice mix to coat. Heat 12-inch nonstick skillet over medium-high heat. Spray skillet with nonstick vegetable cooking spray. Cook chops for 4 to 5 minutes, or until crisp and desired doneness, turning chops over once.

If desired, spoon additional melted butter over chops before serving.

Black and red pepper blend is a prepared spice mix. If it is not available, substitute a combination of 1½ tablespoons medium-grind black pepper and 1½ teaspoons cayenne.

TIP: If cooking meat to well done, reduce heat to medium after chops are crisp on both sides. Continue cooking an additional 1 to 2 minutes, or until meat is no longer pink inside.

Per Serving: Calories: 218 • Protein: 27 g. • Carbohydrate: 7 g. • Fat: 9 g.
• Cholesterol: 111 mg. • Sodium: 1209 mg.
Exchanges: 3 very lean meat, 1¾ fat

Orange-sauced Venison Chops ● VERY FAST

SAUCE:

1 can (14½ oz.) ready-to-serve chicken broth

¼ cup cornstarch

½ teaspoon dried thyme leaves

½ cup frozen orange juice concentrate, defrosted

3 tablespoons orange-flavored liqueur

1 tablespoon grated fresh orange peel

1 tablespoon lemon juice

6 bone-in venison loin chops (6 oz. each), ½ inch thick

6 servings

In 2-quart saucepan, combine broth, cornstarch and thyme. Bring to a boil over high heat, stirring constantly. Boil for 1 minute, stirring constantly. Remove from heat. Stir in remaining sauce ingredients until smooth. Set aside and keep warm.

Spray rack in broiler pan with nonstick vegetable cooking spray. Arrange chops on rack. Broil with surface of chops 4 to 5 inches from heat for 10 to 12 minutes, or until meat is desired doneness, turning chops over once. Serve chops with sauce.

Per Serving: Calories: 224 • Protein: 27 g. • Carbohydrate: 17 g. • Fat: 3 g.
• Cholesterol: 95 mg. • Sodium: 339 mg.
Exchanges: 3 very lean meat, 1 fruit, ¾ fat

Stuffing-topped Venison Chops

4 bone-in venison loin chops
   (6 oz. each), ½ inch thick
½ teaspoon pepper, divided
3 tablespoons butter or
   margarine
2 stalks celery, sliced (1 cup)
1 small onion, chopped (½ cup)
2 tablespoons sesame seed
1 cup ready-to-serve chicken
   broth
2 teaspoons Worcestershire
   sauce
1½ teaspoons dried thyme leaves
¼ to ½ teaspoon salt
4 cups unseasoned dry bread
   cubes (¼-inch cubes)

4 servings

Heat oven to 350°F. Spray 12 × 8-inch baking dish with nonstick vegetable cooking spray. Set aside.

Heat 10-inch nonstick skillet over medium-high heat. Spray skillet with nonstick vegetable cooking spray. Add chops. Cook for 5 to 6 minutes, or until browned, turning chops over once. Arrange chops in single layer in prepared dish. Sprinkle evenly with ¼ teaspoon pepper. Set aside.

Wipe out skillet. In same skillet, melt butter over medium-high heat. Add celery, onion and sesame seed. Cook for 4 to 5 minutes, or until vegetables are tender-crisp, stirring frequently. Remove from heat. Stir in broth, Worcestershire sauce, thyme, salt and remaining ¼ teaspoon pepper. Add bread cubes; toss just until moistened. Spoon mixture over chops. Cover with foil.

Bake for 40 to 45 minutes, or until meat is no longer pink.

Per Serving: Calories: 461 • Protein: 34 g. • Carbohydrate: 41 g. • Fat: 17 g. • Cholesterol: 120 mg. • Sodium: 1083 mg.
Exchanges: 2½ starch, 3 very lean meat, 3½ fat

Grilled Szechuan Steaks 🌶️ FAST LOW-FAT

MARINADE:

¼ cup sliced green onions
1½ tablespoons soy sauce
1 tablespoon lemon juice
1 tablespoon toasted sesame seed
2 teaspoons hot chili sauce with garlic
1 teaspoon sugar
1 teaspoon grated fresh gingerroot
4 boneless venison round steaks (4 oz. each), ¾ to 1 inch thick
¼ teaspoon cornstarch

4 servings

In shallow dish, combine all marinade ingredients. Add steaks, turning to coat. Cover with plastic wrap. Chill 30 minutes, turning steaks over once.

Prepare grill for medium direct heat. Spray cooking grid with non-stick vegetable cooking spray. Drain and reserve marinade from meat. Grill steaks, covered, for 10 to 12 minutes, or until desired doneness, turning steaks over once.

Meanwhile, in 1-quart saucepan, combine reserved marinade and the cornstarch. Bring to a boil over medium-low heat, stirring constantly. Serve as sauce over steaks.

TIP: For more intense flavor, marinate steaks for several hours or overnight.

Per Serving: Calories: 160 • Protein: 26 g.
• Carbohydrate: 4 g. • Fat: 4 g.
• Cholesterol: 95 mg. • Sodium: 454 mg.
Exchanges: 3 very lean meat, ¾ fat

Venison Steaks with Red Pepper Sauce 🌶️ FAST LOW-FAT ↑

1 tablespoon butter or margarine
3 large tomatoes, peeled, seeded and chopped (2 cups)
2 roasted red peppers*, chopped
¾ teaspoon dried oregano leaves
½ teaspoon garlic powder
½ teaspoon paprika
¼ teaspoon cayenne
4 boneless venison loin steaks (4 oz. each), ¾ to 1 inch thick

4 servings

In 1-quart saucepan, melt butter over medium heat. Add tomatoes and peppers. Cook for 3 to 4 minutes, or until tomatoes are soft, stirring frequently. Stir in oregano, garlic powder, paprika and cayenne. Cook for 3 to 5 minutes, or until sauce is thickened, stirring frequently. Set aside and keep warm.

Spray rack in broiler pan with nonstick vegetable cooking spray. Arrange steaks on rack. Broil with surface of steaks 4 to 5 inches from heat for 6 to 8 minutes, or until desired doneness, turning steaks over once. Serve steaks with sauce.

*See Classic Mushroom-Wild Rice Casserole (page 14) for technique for roasting peppers.

Per Serving: Calories: 195 • Protein: 27 g. • Carbohydrate: 7 g. • Fat: 6 g.
• Cholesterol: 103 mg. • Sodium: 162 mg.
Exchanges: 3 very lean meat, 1½ vegetable, 1 fat

Venison with Blue Cheese-Port Sauce ·LOW-FAT·

MARINADE:

1 cup tawny port
1 can (5.5 oz.) spicy vegetable juice
⅓ cup thinly sliced green onions
2 cloves garlic, minced
½ teaspoon coarsely ground pepper
¼ teaspoon ground allspice

1-lb. top round steak, ½ to ¾ inch thick
½ cup beef or venison stock
2 to 4 oz. blue cheese, crumbled

4 servings

In large sealable plastic bag, combine marinade ingredients. Using sharp knife, score steak at 1-inch intervals in crisscross pattern to ⅛-inch depth. Place steak in bag, seal bag and turn to coat steak. Refrigerate 4 hours, turning bag occasionally.

Prepare grill for medium-direct heat. Drain and reserve marinade from steak. Set steak aside. Place marinade in 2-quart saucepan. Bring to a boil over medium-high heat. Boil for 6 to 8 minutes, or until sauce is reduced to 1 cup. Add stock. Return to a boil. Boil for 4 to 6 minutes, or until sauce is reduced to 1 cup again. Stir in cheese. Set sauce aside and keep warm.

Grill steak, covered, for 8 to 10 minutes, or until meat is desired doneness, turning steak over once. Cut steak into slices or serving-size pieces and serve with sauce.

Per Serving: Calories: 257 • Protein: 31 g.
• Carbohydrate: 11 g. • Fat: 9 g.
• Cholesterol: 111 mg. • Sodium: 479 mg.
Exchanges: 3¾ very lean meat,
¾ vegetable, 1¾ fat

Swiss Steak ·LOW-FAT·

2-lb. boneless venison sirloin steak, 1 inch thick, cut into serving-size pieces, or 8 boneless venison loin steaks (4 oz. each), ¾ to 1 inch thick
2 tablespoons dry onion soup mix
½ teaspoon freshly ground pepper
¼ to ½ teaspoon crushed red pepper flakes

1 green pepper, sliced into rings and seeded
1 cup sliced fresh mushrooms
1 can (14½ oz.) diced tomatoes, drained (reserve liquid)
1 tablespoon steak sauce
1 tablespoon cornstarch

8 servings

Heat oven to 350°F. Line 12 × 8-inch baking dish with 12 × 28-inch piece heavy-duty foil. Arrange meat in single layer in dish. Sprinkle meat evenly with soup mix, ground pepper and pepper flakes. Top evenly with green pepper and mushrooms.

Spoon tomatoes over meat. In small bowl, combine reserved tomato liquid and the steak sauce. Stir in cornstarch until smooth. Pour mixture evenly over meat. Fold and crimp foil over meat to enclose. Bake for 1¼ to 1½ hours, or until meat is very tender.

Per Serving: Calories: 166 • Protein: 27 g. • Carbohydrate: 6 g. • Fat: 3 g.
• Cholesterol: 97 mg. • Sodium: 442 mg.
Exchanges: 3 very lean meat, 1¼ vegetable, ½ fat

Jaegermeister-Lemon Steaks 🎱 VERY FAST →

The distinct flavor of Jaegermeister® liqueur is an appropriate partner to the robustness of venison meat. This recipe is for people who like lots of flavor.

4 boneless venison loin steaks
     (4 oz. each), pounded to
     ¹/₂-inch thickness
     Coarsely ground pepper
1 teaspoon salt*
4 tablespoons butter
4 tablespoons Jaegermeister
     liqueur
¹/₄ cup finely chopped onion
¹/₄ cup lemon juice
1 tablespoon snipped fresh
     parsley

4 servings

Generously sprinkle both sides of steaks with pepper and pat pepper into meat. Sprinkle salt evenly in heavy 10-inch skillet. Heat skillet over medium-high heat just until salt begins to brown.

Add steaks. Cook for 1¹/₂ to 2 minutes, or until steaks are well browned on bottom. Turn steaks over. Reduce heat to medium-low. Top each steak with 1 tablespoon butter and sprinkle each with 1 tablespoon Jaegermeister. Add onion to skillet. Cook for 6 to 8 minutes, or until meat is desired doneness, stirring onion occasionally.

Remove steaks from skillet. Set aside and keep warm. Add juice to skillet, stirring to loosen browned bits from bottom of pan. Increase heat to medium. Cook for 2 to 3 minutes, or until sauce is slightly reduced, stirring occasionally. Remove from heat. Stir in parsley. Serve sauce over steaks.

*Coarse salt works best, but table salt is acceptable.

Per Serving: Calories: 286 • Protein: 26 g.
• Carbohydrate: 6 g. • Fat: 14 g.
• Cholesterol: 127 mg. • Sodium: 729 mg.
Exchanges: 3 lean meat, 1¹/₄ vegetable, 1 fat

Seared Mustard Steak 🎱 LOW-FAT

¹/₄ cup beef or venison stock
2 tablespoons Dijon mustard
1 tablespoon finely chopped
     green onion or chives
1 teaspoon Worcestershire sauce

¹/₂ teaspoon dried thyme leaves
4 boneless venison loin steaks
     (4 oz. each), pounded to
     ¹/₄-inch thickness
     Coarsely ground pepper to taste

4 servings

In shallow dish, combine stock, mustard, onion, Worcestershire sauce and thyme. Place steaks in dish, turning to coat. Cover with plastic wrap. Chill 30 minutes, turning steaks over once.

Sprinkle both sides of steaks liberally with pepper. Heat 12-inch non-stick skillet over medium-high heat. Spray skillet with nonstick vegetable cooking spray. Cook for 5 to 6 minutes, or until meat is desired doneness, turning steaks over once. Drizzle remaining marinade over steaks, if desired.

Per Serving: Calories: 149 • Protein: 26 g. • Carbohydrate: 1 g. • Fat: 3 g.
• Cholesterol: 96 mg. • Sodium: 303 mg.
Exchanges: 3 very lean meat, ¹/₂ fat

Old-fashioned
Steaks with Pan Gravy

¼ cup plus 3 tablespoons all-purpose flour, divided
¾ teaspoon freshly ground pepper
½ teaspoon salt
¼ teaspoon paprika
4 boneless venison loin steaks (4 oz. each),
    ¾ to 1 inch thick
3 tablespoons butter or margarine
1¾ cups 1% milk

4 servings

In shallow dish, combine ¼ cup flour, the pepper, salt and paprika. Dredge steaks in flour mixture to coat.

In 12-inch nonstick skillet, melt butter over medium heat. Add steaks. Cook for 6 to 8 minutes, or until browned and desired doneness, turning steaks over once. Remove steaks from skillet and keep warm.

In small mixing bowl, combine milk and remaining 3 tablespoons flour. Stir until smooth. Whisk mixture into drippings in skillet. Cook over medium heat for 2 to 3 minutes, or until gravy bubbles, stirring constantly. Cook for 1 minute longer, stirring constantly. Season to taste with salt and pepper. Serve gravy over steaks.

TIP: If you prefer thinner gravy, add a small amount of milk or water.

Per Serving: Calories: 308 • Protein: 31 g. • Carbohydrate: 16 g. • Fat: 13 g. • Cholesterol: 124 mg. • Sodium: 473 mg.
Exchanges: ¾ starch, 3 very lean meat, ¼ low-fat milk, 2¼ fat

Venison Steaks
with Herb-Mustard Sauce

¼ cup butter, softened
2 tablespoons Dijon mustard
2 tablespoons finely chopped onion
1 tablespoon snipped fresh Italian parsley
1 tablespoon snipped fresh tarragon
1 tablespoon snipped fresh chives
1 clove garlic, minced
8 boneless venison loin steaks
    (4 oz. each), ¾ to 1 inch thick

8 servings

In small mixing bowl, combine butter, mustard, onion, parsley, tarragon, chives and garlic. Set sauce aside.

Spray rack in broiler pan with nonstick vegetable cooking spray. Arrange steaks on rack. Broil with surface of steaks 4 to 5 inches from heat for 6 to 8 minutes, or until desired doneness, turning steaks over once and brushing with sauce once or twice. Serve steaks with any remaining sauce. Garnish with fresh herb sprigs, if desired.

Per Serving: Calories: 191 • Protein: 26 g. • Carbohydrate: <1 g. • Fat: 8 g. • Cholesterol: 111 mg. • Sodium: 195 mg.
Exchanges: 3 very lean meat, 1¾ fat

Jaeger Schnitzel

Schnitzel is the German word for "cutlet" and describes meat that is dipped in egg, breaded and fried. "Jaeger," or "hunter's style," means that the schnitzel is served with a mushroom gravy.

GRAVY:

- 1 tablespoon butter
- 1/4 cup finely chopped shallots
- 8 oz. fresh mushrooms, sliced (3 cups)
- 1/2 cup dry sherry
- 2 cups beef or venison stock
- 1/4 cup all-purpose flour
- 1/4 teaspoon seasoned salt

- 1/3 cup all-purpose flour
- 1/2 teaspoon coarsely ground pepper
- 1/2 teaspoon seasoned salt
- 4 boneless venison loin steaks (4 oz. each), pounded to 1/4-inch thickness
- 2 eggs, lightly beaten
- 1/2 cup dry unseasoned bread crumbs
- 3 tablespoons vegetable oil
- 1 tablespoon lemon juice
  Lemon wedges or slices for garnish

4 servings

For gravy, in 2-quart saucepan, melt butter over medium heat. Add shallots. Cook for 2 to 3 minutes, or until golden, stirring occasionally. Add mushrooms and sherry. Cook for 4 to 5 minutes, or until mushrooms are tender, stirring occasionally.

In 2-cup measure, combine stock and 1/4 cup flour. Gradually stir stock mixture into pan. Cook for 8 to 10 minutes, or until gravy is thickened and bubbly, stirring constantly. Stir in 1/4 teaspoon seasoned salt. Set aside and keep warm.

In shallow dish, combine 1/3 cup flour, the pepper and 1/2 teaspoon seasoned salt. Dredge steaks in flour mixture to coat. Dip steaks in eggs, then dredge in bread crumbs. In 12-inch nonstick skillet, heat oil over medium heat. Cook steaks for 4 to 6 minutes, or until browned, turning steaks over once.

Sprinkle steaks evenly with juice. Serve with gravy and lemon wedges. Garnish with snipped fresh parsley, if desired.

Per Serving: Calories: 478 • Protein: 35 g. • Carbohydrate: 30 g. • Fat: 20 g. • Cholesterol: 210 mg. • Sodium: 836 mg.
Exchanges: 1¾ starch, 3½ very lean meat, 1 vegetable, 4 fat

Mushroom-stuffed Steaks

This recipe makes a larger than normal serving size, but it's worth the splurge for this rich, earthy mushroom stuffing.

3 cups hot water
1 oz. dried porcini mushrooms
1 oz. dried morel mushrooms
3 tablespoons olive oil, divided
⅓ cup finely chopped onion or
    shallots
¼ cup brandy
½ cup dry sherry
½ cup beef or venison stock
1 cup heavy whipping cream
4 boneless venison loin steaks
    (8 oz. each), ¾ to 1 inch
    thick

4 servings

TIPS:

Porcini mushrooms, also known as cèpes, are pungent, meaty mushrooms that can have caps from 1 to 10 inches in diameter.

Morel mushrooms are spongy, honeycombed, cone-shaped wild mushrooms with a smoky, earthy flavor.

In medium mixing bowl, combine hot water and dried mushrooms. Let stand for 15 to 30 minutes, or until mushrooms are soft. Drain liquid, reserving 1 cup. Chop mushrooms, discarding tough stems. Set aside.

In 10-inch skillet, heat 1 tablespoon oil over medium heat. Add onion. Cook for 1 minute, stirring occasionally. Add half of mushrooms. Cook for 3 to 5 minutes, or until mushrooms and onions are golden, stirring occasionally. Set aside.

In 2-quart saucepan, heat 1 tablespoon oil over medium heat. Add remaining mushrooms. Cook for 1 to 2 minutes, or until mushrooms are golden, stirring frequently. Stir in brandy. Bring to a boil over high heat. Boil for 1 to 2 minutes, or until liquid is nearly gone, stirring frequently.

Add sherry, stock and reserved mushroom liquid. Bring to a boil. Boil for 5 minutes, stirring frequently. Stir in cream. Return to a boil, stirring constantly. Reduce heat to medium-low. Simmer for 15 to 20 minutes, or until sauce is thickened, stirring occasionally.

Meanwhile, cut 4-inch-wide and 2-inch-deep pocket in side of each steak. Stuff steaks evenly with mushroom-onion mixture. Secure openings with wooden picks. In 12-inch skillet, heat remaining 1 tablespoon oil over medium heat. Add steaks. Cook for 6 to 8 minutes, or until desired doneness, turning steaks over once. Serve sauce over steaks.

Per Serving: Calories: 626 • Protein: 54 g. • Carbohydrate: 14 g. • Fat: 38 g.
• Cholesterol: 272 mg. • Sodium: 225 mg.
Exchanges: 6 very lean meat, 2½ vegetable, 7½ fat

Venison Wellington

4 boneless venison loin steaks
    (4 oz. each), pounded to
    ¹⁄₂-inch thickness
2 tablespoons Cognac or brandy
1 teaspoon freshly ground pepper
1 tablespoon butter
8 oz. fresh mushrooms, chopped
    (3 cups)
¹⁄₂ cup finely chopped shallots
    or onion
1 egg, separated
2 tablespoons skim milk
1 sheet frozen puff pastry,
    defrosted (half of
    17¹⁄₄-oz. pkg.)

4 servings

Per Serving: Calories: 577 • Protein: 34 g.
• Carbohydrate: 36 g. • Fat: 31 g.
• Cholesterol: 156 mg. • Sodium: 252 mg.
Exchanges: 2 starch, 3¹⁄₂ very lean meat,
1 vegetable, 6 fat

Heat 12-inch nonstick skillet over medium heat. Spray with nonstick vegetable cooking spray. Add steaks. Cook for 4 to 5 minutes, or until browned, turning steaks over once. Place steaks in shallow dish. Sprinkle steaks evenly with Cognac and pepper. Set aside.

Wipe out skillet. In same skillet, melt butter over medium heat. Add mushrooms and shallots. Cook for 8 to 10 minutes, or until vegetables are golden brown, stirring frequently. Remove from skillet and cool slightly.

In small mixing bowl, slightly beat egg white. Set aside. In second bowl, beat egg yolk with milk. Set aside.

Heat oven to 425°F. Spray baking sheet with nonstick vegetable cooking spray. Set aside. On lightly floured surface, roll pastry into 12-inch square. Cut into four 6-inch squares. Spoon ¹⁄₄ of mushroom mixture onto center of each square. Top with steaks. Brush edges of pastry with beaten egg white. Fold two opposite sides together over steaks, pinching to seal. Pinch ends to seal, and tuck under packets. Place pastry packets on prepared baking sheet. Brush packets with egg yolk mixture.

Bake for 10 minutes. Reduce oven temperature to 350°F. Bake for 8 to 10 minutes longer, or until packets are golden brown. Let stand for 5 minutes before serving.

TIP: If desired, trim a small amount of pastry from rolled-out square. Roll out trimmed piece and cut out decorative shapes, such as leaves, to place on packets before baking.

Venison Medallions with Apples

2 tablespoons butter or margarine
2 large cooking apples, cored and
    thinly sliced
¼ cup dry sherry
¼ cup golden raisins
1 cup packed brown sugar
½ cup applejack brandy
½ cup apple cider or apple juice
2 teaspoons cooking oil
6 boneless venison loin steaks
    (4 oz. each), ¾ to 1 inch thick

6 servings

Per Serving: Calories: 449 • Protein: 26 g.
• Carbohydrate: 58 g. • Fat: 8 g.
• Cholesterol: 106 mg. • Sodium: 101 mg.
Exchanges: 3 very lean meat, 4 fruit, 1¾ fat

In 10-inch skillet, melt butter over medium heat. Add apple slices, sherry and raisins. Cook for 5 to 6 minutes, or until apples are tender-crisp, stirring occasionally. Remove from heat; set aside.

In 1-quart saucepan, combine sugar, brandy and apple cider. Cook over medium-high heat for 2 to 3 minutes, or until sugar dissolves and mixture boils, stirring constantly. Boil for 2 minutes, stirring frequently. Set syrup aside.

In 12-inch nonstick skillet, heat oil over medium-high heat. Add steaks. Cook for 5 to 6 minutes, or until meat is browned, turning steaks over once. Drain. Pour syrup over meat. Bring to a boil. Cover. Reduce heat to low. Simmer for 5 to 10 minutes, or until meat is desired doneness.

Remove steaks from skillet and place on serving platter. Spoon apple slices and raisins around steaks. Strain meat cooking liquid through fine-mesh sieve. Spoon half of liquid over steaks and apples. Serve remaining liquid on the side.

Steps with Mustard Sauce

4 boneless venison loin steaks
    (4 oz. each), pounded to
    ¼-inch thickness
    Salt and pepper to taste
1 tablespoon butter
¼ cup finely chopped onion
2 cups beef or venison stock
2 tablespoons cornstarch
¼ cup snipped fresh marjoram,
    parsley or thyme*
¼ cup Dijon mustard
2 tablespoons lemon juice
1 teaspoon Worcestershire
    sauce
3 tablespoons Madeira wine
    Fresh herb sprigs for garnish

4 servings

Heat 12-inch nonstick skillet over medium heat. Spray with nonstick vegetable cooking spray. Add steaks. Cook for 3 to 4 minutes, or until meat is desired doneness, turning steaks over once. Remove steaks to serving platter. Sprinkle with salt and pepper. Set aside and keep warm.

In same skillet, melt butter over medium heat. Add onion. Cook for 2 to 3 minutes, or until onion is tender, stirring occasionally. In medium mixing bowl, combine stock and cornstarch. Stir stock mixture, fresh herbs, mustard, juice and Worcestershire sauce into skillet. Cook for 2 to 3 minutes, or until sauce thickens and bubbles, stirring constantly. Stir in Madeira. Cook for 1 minute. Spoon sauce over steaks and garnish with fresh herb sprigs.

A combination of fresh herbs equaling ¼ cup may also be used.

Per Serving: Calories: 227 • Protein: 27 g. • Carbohydrate: 7 g. • Fat: 6 g.
• Cholesterol: 104 mg. • Sodium: 824 mg.
Exchanges: 3 very lean meat, 1¼ fat

Peppercorn Tenderloin

3 cloves garlic, minced
1-lb. venison tenderloin
1 to 2 tablespoons coarsely
    crushed whole peppercorns*
1 tablespoon butter

4 servings

Heat oven to 425°F. Spray 13 × 9-inch baking pan with nonstick vegetable cooking spray. Set aside.

Spread garlic evenly over tenderloin. Roll tenderloin in crushed peppercorns to coat, pressing peppercorns into meat. Place tenderloin in prepared pan. Bake for 10 minutes. Dot tenderloin with butter. Continue baking for 6 to 10 minutes, or until tenderloin is desired doneness. Let tenderloin stand, tented with foil, for 5 minutes before slicing.

For a more colorful dish, use a blend with red, black and green peppercorns.

Per Serving: Calories: 173 • Protein: 26 g.
• Carbohydrate: 2 g. • Fat: 6 g.
• Cholesterol: 104 mg. • Sodium: 89 mg.
Exchanges: 3 very lean meat, 1 fat

Cantonese Venison Tenderloin LOW-FAT

MARINADE:
- ¼ cup rice wine vinegar
- ¼ cup hoisin sauce
- 3 tablespoons dry sherry
- 2 tablespoons soy sauce
- 2 tablespoons sesame oil
- ¼ cup sliced green onions
- 3 cloves garlic, minced
- 1 tablespoon grated fresh gingerroot or 1 teaspoon ground ginger

- 1-lb. venison tenderloin
- 1 teaspoon cornstarch

4 servings

In 2-cup measure, combine vinegar, hoisin sauce, sherry, soy sauce and oil. Whisk to blend. Stir in remaining marinade ingredients. Reserve ½ cup marinade. Place tenderloin in large, sealable plastic bag. Add marinade, seal bag and turn to coat tenderloin. Refrigerate 2 to 3 hours, turning bag occasionally.

In 1-quart saucepan, combine reserved marinade and the cornstarch. Cook over high heat for 2 to 3 minutes, or until sauce thickens and bubbles, stirring constantly. Set aside.

Drain and discard marinade from meat. Prepare grill for medium direct heat. Spray cooking grid with nonstick vegetable cooking spray. Grill tenderloin for 15 to 20 minutes, or until meat is desired doneness, turning tenderloin two or three times and brushing with sauce during last half of cooking. Let tenderloin stand, tented with foil, for 5 minutes before slicing.

Per Serving: Calories: 238 • Protein: 26 g.
• Carbohydrate: 10 g. • Fat: 8 g.
• Cholesterol: 95 mg. • Sodium: 673 mg.
Exchanges: 3 very lean meat, 1½ fat

Steak Oscar ↑

- 1-lb. venison tenderloin
- ¼ teaspoon pepper
- ½ cup water
- 1 lb. fresh asparagus spears, trimmed to 4-inch lengths

- 1 pkg. (0.9 oz.) Béarnaise sauce mix
- 4 oz. crabmeat*, flaked

6 servings

Cut tenderloin crosswise into 6 equal pieces, approximately 1½ inches thick. Press pieces to flatten slightly. Sprinkle pieces evenly with pepper. Spray rack in broiler pan with nonstick vegetable cooking spray. Arrange steaks on rack. Set aside.

In 1-quart saucepan, bring water to a boil over high heat. Add asparagus. Reduce heat to medium. Cook for 3 to 4 minutes, or until asparagus is tender-crisp. Drain. Set aside.

Prepare Béarnaise sauce as directed on package. Keep warm.

Broil steaks 3 to 4 inches from heat for 5 minutes. Turn steaks over and broil for 3 minutes longer. Remove from heat. Top steaks evenly with crabmeat, then asparagus. Return to broiler. Broil for 2 to 3 minutes, or until heated through. Spoon sauce over steaks.

*Imitation crabmeat may be substituted for real crabmeat.

Per Serving: Calories: 232 • Protein: 24 g. • Carbohydrate: 8 g. • Fat: 11 g.
• Cholesterol: 109 mg. • Sodium: 353 mg.
Exchanges: 3 very lean meat, 2¼ fat

Sun-dried Tomato-Basil Tenderloin ◆LOW-FAT

½ cup hot water
 1 oz. dry-pack sun-dried
    tomatoes, coarsely snipped
¼ cup snipped fresh basil
 1-lb. venison tenderloin
¼ teaspoon freshly ground pepper

4 servings

Per Serving: Calories: 159 • Protein: 27 g.
• Carbohydrate: 5 g. • Fat: 3 g.
• Cholesterol: 95 mg. • Sodium: 53 mg.
Exchanges: 3 very lean meat, 1 vegetable,
½ fat

In small mixing bowl, combine water and tomatoes. Soak for 30 minutes to soften tomatoes. Drain. Add basil to tomatoes. Mix well.

Prepare grill for medium direct heat. Spray cooking grid with non-stick vegetable cooking spray. Make a horizontal cut through center of tenderloin to within ½ inch of opposite side; do not cut through. Open tenderloin like a book. Spoon and pack tomato mixture down one side of tenderloin. Fold other side of tenderloin over to enclose stuffing. Tie tenderloin with kitchen string at 1½-inch intervals. Sprinkle tenderloin evenly with pepper.

Grill tenderloin, covered, for 16 to 20 minutes, or until desired doneness, turning tenderloin two or three times. Let tenderloin stand, tented with foil, for 5 minutes before slicing.

Roasting large cuts of venison can be done using either dry-heat or moist-heat cooking techniques. Dry-heat roasting includes both high- and low-temperature methods. Most moist-heat roasting is done by braising, which includes pot roasting.

Use only prime cuts, such as top round, sirloin tip, backstrap and rump roasts, for dry-heat roasting. These cuts are naturally tender and do not need long, slow cooking to tenderize them.

For high-temperature cooking, select a roast between 2 and 5 inches thick, or a thinner piece that has been rolled and tied. Often, you should first brown the meat in a skillet or Dutch oven in hot oil, then roast it in a 400° to 450°F oven. Roasts should only be cooked rare to medium when done this way. Roasts cooked to well done will dry out and shrink at high temperatures.

Use a meat thermometer or an instant-read thermometer to check doneness of roasts. Remove the roast from the oven when the thermometer reads 5°F below the desired temperature in the thickest part of the roast. The internal temperature of the roasts will go up about 5°F in the 10 minutes after the roast is removed from the oven.

Low-temperature roasting can be used for prime cuts as well as less tender cuts, such as the bottom round, which need longer cooking to ensure tenderness. Cover the meat with bacon, or beef or pork fat (available from meat cutters), or baste it frequently, when cooking in a slow (300° to 325°F) oven. At low heats, roasts may be cooked to rare, medium or well done.

Moist-heat cooking is used to tenderize tougher cuts, such as shoulder roasts, and also works with medium-tender cuts. Brown the roast in hot oil, then add liquid and flavorings and cover the pan tightly. Cook the meat until tender, either on the stove top or in a moderate (325° to 350°F) oven. When pot roasting, add vegetables during the last hour or so of cooking. Braised meat is always served well done.

Internal Temperature Doneness Chart

DONENESS	INTERNAL TEMPERATURE
Rare	130° to 135°F
Medium-rare	135° to 140°F
Medium	140° to 145°F
Medium-well	150° to 155°F
Well done	155° to 160°F

Roast Boneless Sirloin Tip
(High-temperature Roasting) LOW-FAT

1 to 2 tablespoons olive oil or vegetable oil
1 boneless venison sirloin tip, rolled top round or rump roast, 2 to 5 inches thick

2 to 4 servings per lb.

Heat oven to 450°F. In medium skillet or Dutch oven, heat oil over medium-high heat. Add roast and sear it on all sides. Place roast on rack in roasting pan. Roast to desired doneness (see chart above), 20 to 30 minutes per lb. Remove roast from oven when internal temperature is 5°F less than desired. Let meat rest for 10 minutes before carving.

Per Serving: Calories: 146 • Protein: 26 g. • Carbohydrate: 0 g. • Fat: 4 g. • Cholesterol: 95 mg. • Sodium: 46 mg.
Exchanges: 3 very lean meat, ¾ fat

Peppered Venison Roast
(Low-temperature Roasting)

1 venison sirloin tip, rolled top round, bottom round or rump roast, 3 to 5 lbs.
1 tablespoon vegetable oil
   Coarsely cracked black pepper
8 to 10 slices bacon

2 to 4 servings per lb.

Heat oven to 325°F. Place roast on rack in roasting pan. Brush roast evenly with oil; sprinkle liberally with pepper. Cover roast with bacon slices. Roast to desired doneness (see chart above), 20 to 30 minutes per lb. Remove roast from oven when internal temperature is 5°F less than desired. Let meat rest for 10 minutes before carving. Serve with pan juices.

Per Serving: Calories: 213 • Protein: 27 g. • Carbohydrate: 0 g. • Fat: 11 g. • Cholesterol: 104 mg. • Sodium: 133 mg.
Exchanges: 3¼ very lean meat, 2 fat

Grilled Garlic-Rosemary Roast *LOW-FAT*

MARINADE:

1½ cups dry red wine
½ cup packed brown sugar
½ oz. fresh rosemary sprigs, cut into 1-inch pieces (½ cup)
4 to 5 cloves garlic, crushed
½ teaspoon freshly ground pepper

2-lb. venison top round roast, 1½ to 2 inches thick

6 to 8 servings

In 4-cup measure, combine all marinade ingredients. Stir to dissolve sugar. Place roast in large sealable plastic bag. Add marinade, seal bag and turn to coat roast. Refrigerate roast several hours or overnight, turning bag occasionally.

Prepare grill for medium direct heat. Drain and reserve marinade from roast. Strain marinade through fine-mesh sieve, if desired. Grill roast, covered, for 30 to 40 minutes for medium-rare, or until desired doneness (see chart, opposite), turning roast and basting with reserved marinade every 10 minutes. Tent with foil. Let roast stand for 10 minutes before carving.

Per Serving: Calories: 224 • Protein: 26 g. • Carbohydrate: 15 g. • Fat: 3 g.
• Cholesterol: 95 mg. • Sodium: 54 mg.
Exchanges: 3 very lean meat, ½ fat

← Hunter's Venison Roast LOW-FAT

RUB:
- 6 juniper berries, crushed
- 1 teaspoon dried marjoram leaves
- 1 teaspoon dried thyme leaves
- 1 teaspoon salt
- 1/2 teaspoon freshly ground pepper

- 2-lb. venison top round roast
- 1 tablespoon vegetable oil
- 1 medium onion, chopped (1 cup)
- 1 cup dry red wine
- 2 tablespoons plus 1 teaspoon red wine vinegar, divided
- 1/2 cup half-and-half
- 1 tablespoon red currant jelly

6 to 8 servings

In small bowl, combine all rub ingredients. Pat roast dry with paper towels. Press and spread rub mixture on all sides of roast. Place roast in sealable plastic bag. Refrigerate several hours or overnight.

Heat oven to 350°F. In 6-quart Dutch oven, heat oil over medium-high heat. Add roast and cook for 5 to 6 minutes, or until browned on all sides, turning roast occasionally. Add onion, wine and 2 tablespoons vinegar to Dutch oven. Roast to desired doneness (see chart on page 54), 20 to 30 minutes per lb., basting occasionally with pan juices. Remove roast from pan. Tent with foil. Set aside.

Strain pan juices through fine-mesh sieve. Return juices to Dutch oven. Bring to a boil over medium-high heat. Simmer for 8 to 10 minutes, or until liquid is reduced to 1/4 cup. Stir in half-and-half, jelly and remaining 1 teaspoon vinegar. Cook for 1 to 2 minutes, or until sauce is hot and smooth. Serve sauce over sliced roast.

Per Serving: Calories: 189 • Protein: 27 g. • Carbohydrate: 5 g. • Fat: 6 g. • Cholesterol: 102 mg. • Sodium: 342 mg. Exchanges: 3 very lean meat, 1 1/4 fat

Barbecued Venison Roast LOW-FAT ↑

- 2 cans (12 oz. each) carbonated cola beverage
- 2/3 cup Worcestershire sauce
- 3 to 4-lb. venison top or bottom round roast
- 1 medium onion, sliced
- 1/2 cup water
- 1/4 to 1/2 teaspoon pepper
- 1/2 to 1 cup barbecue sauce

12 to 16 servings

In large sealable plastic bag, combine cola and Worcestershire sauce. Add roast, seal bag and turn to coat roast. Refrigerate at least 4 hours, turning roast occasionally.

Heat oven to 325°F. Spray roasting pan with nonstick vegetable cooking spray. Drain and discard marinade from roast. Place roast in pan. Add onion and water to pan. Sprinkle roast evenly with pepper. Cover with lid or foil. Bake for 2 1/2 to 3 1/2 hours, or until meat is tender, basting two or three times with pan juices. Let roast stand, covered, for 10 minutes. Drain and discard liquid from pan.

Cut roast into thin slices. Return to pan. Pour barbecue sauce over meat. Bake, covered, for 20 to 30 minutes, or until hot. Serve meat over mashed potatoes, on hamburger buns or on toast.

Per Serving: Calories: 151 • Protein: 26 g. • Carbohydrate: 3 g. • Fat: 3 g. • Cholesterol: 95 mg. • Sodium: 157 mg. Exchanges: 3 very lean meat, 1/2 fat

Sweet & Sour Venison Pot Roast *LOW-FAT*

 1 tablespoon vegetable oil
 4-lb. venison chuck roast, tied if
     necessary
 2 large onions, sliced
 ¼ cup sugar
 ¼ cup honey
 ¼ cup lemon juice
 ½ teaspoon grated lemon peel
 ¼ teaspoon ground cloves
 1 teaspoon salt
 ½ teaspoon freshly ground pepper
 3 medium carrots, cut into 2-inch
     pieces
 1 lb. red potatoes, cut into 2-inch
     pieces

8 servings

Per Serving: Calories: 426 • Protein: 54 g.
• Carbohydrate: 34 g. • Fat: 7 g.
• Cholesterol: 193 mg. • Sodium: 409 mg.
Exchanges: ½ starch, 6 very lean meat,
1½ vegetable, 1½ fat

Heat oven to 325°F. In 6-quart Dutch oven, heat oil over medium-high heat. Add roast. Cook roast for 7 to 10 minutes, or until browned on all sides, turning frequently. Remove from heat. Drain. Add onions.

In 2-cup measure, combine sugar, honey, juice, peel and cloves. Pour mixture over roast and onions. Sprinkle roast evenly with salt and pepper. Cover tightly.

Roast for 1 hour, basting occasionally with pan juices. Add carrots and potatoes, pushing them into the pan juices. Continue roasting for 1½ to 2 hours, or until meat and vegetables are tender. Serve roast with pan juices.

TIPS:

For a reduced sauce, remove roast and vegetables from Dutch oven. Boil pan juices over medium-high heat until desired consistency.

To make gravy from pan juice, strain 2 cups liquid from pan juices; discard remainder. Return 2 cups liquid to Dutch oven. In 1-cup measure, combine ¼ cup all-purpose flour and ⅓ cup water. Gradually whisk flour mixture into pan juices. Bring to a boil over medium-high heat. Cook for 1 to 1½ minutes, or until thickened, stirring constantly. Add salt and pepper to taste.

Apricot-Walnut Stuffed Rolled Roast

STUFFING:

- 4 slices whole-grain bread, cut into ½-inch cubes (2 cups)
- ½ cup chopped walnuts
- 1 tablespoon butter or margarine
- 1 medium onion, chopped (1 cup)
- 1 stalk celery, chopped (½ cup)
- ½ cup chopped dried apricots
- 1 tablespoon dried parsley flakes
- 1 teaspoon dried thyme leaves
- ½ teaspoon salt
- ¼ teaspoon pepper
- ½ to ¾ cup beef or venison stock

- 2 to 3-lb. boneless venison hindquarter roast, butterflied to 1-inch thickness
- 4 slices bacon, halved

8 to 12 servings

Heat oven to 350°F. Spread bread cubes and walnuts in single layer on large baking sheet. Bake for 8 to 10 minutes, or until cubes are toasted and walnuts are lightly browned, stirring once or twice. Set aside. Reduce oven temperature to 325°F.

In 12-inch nonstick skillet, melt butter over medium heat. Add onion and celery. Cook for 3 to 5 minutes, or until vegetables are tender, stirring occasionally. Remove from heat. Stir in bread cubes, walnuts and remaining stuffing ingredients, except stock. Stir in stock just until stuffing is moistened.

See directions at right for rolling roast.

Roast to desired doneness (see chart on page 54), 20 to 25 minutes per lb. Remove and discard bacon slices.

Per Serving: Calories: 210 • Protein: 23 g. • Carbohydrate: 10 g. • Fat: 8 g. • Cholesterol: 83 mg. • Sodium: 241 mg. Exchanges: ½ starch, 2½ very lean meat, ½ vegetable, 1¾ fat

How to Roll Up Apricot-Walnut Stuffed Rolled Roast

SPREAD and pack stuffing evenly on roast. Roll up roast jelly-roll-style, rolling with grain of meat.

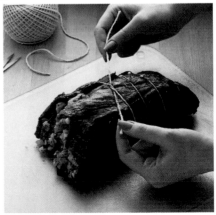

TIE roast at 1-inch intervals, using kitchen string. Place roast on rack in roasting pan. Top evenly with bacon slices. Continue with directions at left.

Venison Roast with Blueberry-Maple Sauce

2-lb. boneless venison loin roast
2 cloves garlic, slivered
1 tablespoon vegetable oil
Coarsely ground pepper
½ teaspoon salt

SAUCE:
1½ cups dry red wine
¼ cup finely chopped shallots
　　or onion
1 cup beef or venison stock
½ cup dried blueberries
3 tablespoons butter, softened
2 to 3 tablespoons maple syrup
½ teaspoon rubbed sage
Salt and pepper to taste

8 servings

Heat oven to 450°F. Make shallow slits in roast with tip of sharp knife. Insert garlic sliver into each slit. Place roast on rack in roasting pan. Brush with oil. Sprinkle roast with pepper. Roast for 10 minutes. Reduce heat to 350°F. Roast to desired doneness (see chart on page 54), 20 to 30 minutes per lb. Sprinkle roast with salt.

Meanwhile, in 2-quart saucepan, combine wine and shallots. Bring to a boil over medium-high heat. Reduce heat to medium. Simmer for 8 to 10 minutes, or until liquid is reduced by half. Stir in stock and blueberries. Return to a simmer. Simmer for 8 to 10 minutes, or until liquid is again reduced by half, stirring occasionally. (For a thicker sauce, stir in 1 teaspoon cornstarch mixed with 1 teaspoon water at this point.)

Whisk in butter, 1 tablespoon at a time. Stir in syrup, sage, salt and pepper. Serve sauce with roast.

Per Serving: Calories: 254 • Protein: 26 g. • Carbohydrate: 16 g. • Fat: 9 g. • Cholesterol: 107 mg. • Sodium: 333 mg.
Exchanges: 3 lean meat, ⅔ fruit

60

Corn-stuffed Rolled Top Round Roast

STUFFING:

  2 tablespoons butter or margarine
  1 small onion, finely chopped (¾ cup)
 ½ cup finely chopped red pepper
  1 cup frozen corn kernels, defrosted
  1 can (4 oz.) minced green chilies
1½ cups crumbled corn bread
 ½ cup shredded Cheddar cheese
 ¼ cup snipped fresh cilantro leaves
 ½ teaspoon cumin seed
 ½ teaspoon salt
 ¼ to ½ teaspoon crushed red pepper flakes

  2 to 3-lb. boneless venison top round roast,
     butterflied to 1-inch thickness
  1 tablespoon vegetable oil

8 to 12 servings

Heat oven to 450°F. In 12-inch skillet, melt butter over medium heat. Add onion and pepper. Cook for 3 to 5 minutes, or until vegetables are tender, stirring occasionally. Stir in corn and chilies. Cook for 1 to 2 minutes, or until corn is heated through, stirring frequently. Remove from heat.

Stir in remaining stuffing ingredients. Spread and pack stuffing evenly on roast. Roll up roast jelly-roll-style, rolling with grain of meat. Tie roast at 1-inch intervals, using kitchen string. Place roast on rack in roasting pan. Brush with oil.

Roast for 10 minutes. Reduce heat to 350°F. Roast to desired doneness (see chart on page 54), 20 to 25 minutes per lb.

TIP: See rolling directions for stuffed roast on page 59.

Per Serving: Calories: 217 • Protein: 24 g. • Carbohydrate: 11 g. • Fat: 8 g. • Cholesterol: 97 mg. • Sodium: 334 mg.
Exchanges: ½ starch, 3 very lean meat, ¼ vegetable, 1¾ fat

Soups, Stews & Chilies

Venison Stock ^{LOW-FAT}

Many recipes in this book call for stock or broth. Ready-to-serve beef broth is available in cans, but for the best quality and flavor, make your own stock with the large bones from your deer. Browning the bones in the oven makes the stock rich and dark. Long cooking helps to bring out the flavors. Do not add salt to your stock. Salt should be added to the recipe in which the stock is used in order to best control the recipe's flavor.

2 lbs. well-trimmed venison bones with bits of meat	1 tablespoon margarine or butter
1 tablespoon vegetable oil	1 cup boiling water
2 medium carrots, cut into 1-inch pieces (1 cup)	14 cups cold water
2 stalks celery, cut into 1-inch pieces (1 cup)	1 tablespoon no-salt-added tomato paste
1 medium onion, cut into 1-inch chunks (1 cup)	2 whole cloves garlic, peeled
	2 sprigs fresh parsley
	1 sprig fresh thyme
	1 bay leaf

8 cups

Heat oven to 375°F. Cut most meat from bones. Cut meat into chunks. Place meat and bones in 13 × 9-inch roasting pan. Drizzle oil evenly over meat and bones, stirring to coat. Bake for 45 minutes to 1 hour, or until meat is well browned, stirring occasionally. Drain and discard fat from pan.

Meanwhile, combine carrots, celery, onion and margarine in 8-quart stock-pot. Cook over medium heat for 12 to 16 minutes, or until vegetables are tender-crisp and onion is golden brown, stirring occasionally.

Transfer browned meat and bones to stockpot. Pour boiling water into roasting pan, scraping bottom to loosen browned bits. Pour mixture into stockpot. Add remaining ingredients to stockpot. Bring to a simmer over medium-high heat, skimming surface of stock frequently.

Reduce heat to medium-low. Simmer, partially covered, for 4 hours, skimming occasionally and adding additional hot water as needed to keep meat and vegetables covered. Strain and discard solids from stock. Add enough additional water to stock to equal 8 cups. Cool. Cover. Chill overnight.

Skim any fat from surface of stock. Freeze any stock not immediately used, in premeasured amounts, in small plastic food-storage bags or containers.

TIP: If freezing stock in plastic food-storage bags, freeze bags flat so they will be easier to store in the freezer.

Per Serving: Calories: 43 • Protein: 5 g. • Carbohydrate: 3 g. • Fat: 2 g.
• Cholesterol: 0 mg. • Sodium: 80 mg.
Exchanges: ½ very lean meat, ½ vegetable, ¼ fat

Sweet Potato & Venison Soup ^{FAST} ^{LOW-FAT} →

1 tablespoon garlic-flavored vegetable oil or olive oil
1 lb. venison top round, cut into ½-inch cubes
6 cups beef or venison stock
1 medium onion, chopped (1 cup)
2 tablespoons Worcestershire sauce
1 teaspoon dried thyme leaves
1 bay leaf
½ teaspoon dried marjoram leaves
½ teaspoon salt
½ teaspoon freshly ground pepper
2 cups cubed peeled sweet potato, ½-inch cubes
1 pkg. (16 oz.) frozen mixed vegetables
½ cup frozen corn kernels
⅓ cup all-purpose flour mixed with ½ cup water

6 to 8 servings

In 6-quart Dutch oven or stockpot, heat oil over medium-high heat. Add venison. Cook for 4 to 6 minutes, or until meat is no longer pink, stirring frequently. Drain. Add stock, onion, Worcestershire sauce, thyme, bay leaf, marjoram, salt and pepper. Bring to a boil over high heat. Cover. Reduce heat to medium-low. Simmer for 30 minutes.

Stir in sweet potato, frozen vegetables and corn. Bring to a boil over medium-high heat. Gradually blend in flour mixture. Reduce heat to medium-low. Cover. Simmer for 10 to 12 minutes, or until vegetables are tender, stirring occasionally. Remove and discard bay leaf.

Per Serving: Calories: 205 • Protein: 17 g.
• Carbohydrate: 27 g. • Fat: 4 g.
• Cholesterol: 48 mg. • Sodium: 445 mg.
Exchanges: 1½ starch, 1½ very lean meat, ½ vegetable, ½ fat

French Onion Soup with Venison

← French Onion Soup
with Venison

2 tablespoons butter, softened, divided
1 large onion, sliced (2 cups)
8 oz. venison top round steak, cut into 1 × ½-inch strips
2 cans (10½ oz. each) concentrated beef broth
1¼ cups water
2 tablespoons Worcestershire sauce
1 clove garlic, minced
6 slices French bread, cut ¾ inch thick
2 tablespoons shredded fresh Parmesan cheese

6 servings

In 3-quart saucepan, melt 1 tablespoon butter over medium heat. Add onion. Cook for 3 minutes, stirring frequently. Reduce heat to low. Continue cooking for 8 to 12 minutes, or until onion is browned, stirring occasionally. Remove onion from pan. Set aside.

Add venison strips to pan. Increase heat to medium. Cook for 2 to 4 minutes, or until meat is no longer pink, stirring occasionally. Add broth, water, Worcestershire sauce and onion. Cook for 10 to 15 minutes, or until hot.

Meanwhile, in small bowl, combine remaining 1 tablespoon butter and the garlic. Spread mixture evenly on both sides of bread slices. Broil slices 4 to 5 inches from heat for 3 to 5 minutes, or until golden brown, turning slices over once. Top slices evenly with Parmesan cheese. Broil for 1 to 2 minutes, or until cheese is melted. Top individual servings of soup with 1 piece garlic toast.

Per Serving: Calories: 231 • Protein: 16 g.
• Carbohydrate: 26 g. • Fat: 7 g.
• Cholesterol: 49 mg. • Sodium: 1099 mg.
Exchanges: 1¼ starch, 1½ very lean meat, 1 vegetable, 1¼ fat

Mediterranean Stew *LOW-FAT*

3 tablespoons olive oil, divided
2 medium onions, sliced (2½ cups)
3 cloves garlic, minced
2 lbs. venison loin roast, cut into 1-inch cubes
¼ cup all-purpose flour
3½ cups beef or venison stock
¾ cup dry red wine
¼ cup lemon juice
1 bay leaf
1 teaspoon dried rosemary leaves, crushed

½ teaspoon dried thyme leaves
¼ teaspoon pepper
2 medium fennel bulbs (10 oz. each), trimmed and sliced
8 oz. fresh mushrooms, sliced (3 cups)
¼ cup snipped fresh parsley
¼ cup chopped Kalamata olives (optional)
2 teaspoons grated lemon peel
½ teaspoon salt (optional)

6 to 8 servings

In 6-quart Dutch oven or stockpot, heat 1 tablespoon oil over medium heat. Add onions and garlic. Cook for 3 to 5 minutes, or until tender, stirring occasionally. Using slotted spoon, transfer onions to bowl. Set aside.

Increase heat to medium-high. In same pot, heat 1 tablespoon oil. Add venison. Cook for 4 to 6 minutes, or until meat is no longer pink, stirring occasionally. Using slotted spoon, transfer venison to bowl with onions. Set aside.

Add remaining 1 tablespoon oil to pot. Stir in flour. Gradually, blend in stock, wine and juice, whisking until smooth. Stir in bay leaf, rosemary, thyme and pepper. Bring to a boil. Boil for 1 minute, stirring constantly. Return onions and venison to pot. Return to a boil. Cover. Reduce heat to low. Simmer for 1 hour, stirring occasionally.

Stir in fennel and mushrooms. Increase heat to medium. Cook, uncovered, for 30 to 40 minutes, or until vegetables are tender and stew is thickened, stirring occasionally. Stir in parsley, olives, peel and salt. Remove and discard bay leaf. Garnish with chopped Roma tomatoes, if desired.

Per Serving: Calories: 243 • Protein: 29 g. • Carbohydrate: 11 g. • Fat: 8 g.
• Cholesterol: 97 mg. • Sodium: 479 mg.
Exchanges: ⅓ starch, 3 very lean meat, 1¼ vegetable, 1¾ fat

Texas Red Chili LOW-FAT

Arguments abound as to what makes a good chili, but any self-respecting Texas chili is devoid of beans and uses cut-up steak instead of ground meat. This recipe tries to stay true to the Texas tradition.

1	tablespoon olive oil
1	medium onion, chopped (1 cup)
1	medium green pepper, seeded and chopped (1 cup)
2	cloves garlic, minced
1	can (28 oz.) diced tomatoes, undrained
1	can (8 oz.) tomato sauce
1	can (4 oz.) chopped green chilies
¼	cup plus 2 tablespoons tomato paste
1	to 2 tablespoons diced canned jalapeño peppers (optional)
1½	tablespoons chili powder
2	teaspoons cocoa
1½	teaspoons dried oregano leaves
1½	teaspoons ground cumin
½	teaspoon ground cinnamon
½	teaspoon salt
½	teaspoon freshly ground pepper
1	lb. venison bottom round steak, cut into 1 × ½ × ¼-inch strips
	Shredded Cheddar cheese (optional)
	Sour cream (optional)

4 to 6 servings

In 4-quart saucepan, heat oil over medium heat. Add onion, green pepper and garlic. Cook for 5 to 7 minutes, or until vegetables are tender, stirring occasionally. Add remaining ingredients, except venison strips, cheese and sour cream. Set aside.

Meanwhile, spray 12-inch nonstick skillet with nonstick vegetable cooking spray. Heat skillet over medium-high heat. Add venison strips. Cook for 4 to 6 minutes, or until meat is no longer pink, stirring occasionally. Drain.

Add meat to saucepan. Mix well. Bring to a boil over medium-high heat. Reduce heat to medium-low. Simmer for 30 to 45 minutes, or until flavors are blended and chili is desired thickness, stirring occasionally. Garnish individual servings with cheese and sour cream.

TIP: If desired, add a can of rinsed and drained red kidney beans to chili.

Per Serving: Calories: 194 • Protein: 21 g. • Carbohydrate: 18 g. • Fat: 5 g. • Cholesterol: 64 mg. • Sodium: 923 mg.
Exchanges: 2 very lean meat, 3¾ vegetable, 1 fat

Black Bean Chili 🔵 LOW-FAT

2 tablespoons vegetable oil, divided
2½ lbs. venison chuck roast, cut into ¾-inch cubes
1 large onion, chopped (1½ cups)
1 cup chopped red pepper
6 cloves garlic, minced
2 cans (14½ oz. each) diced tomatoes, undrained
2 cans (15 oz. each) black beans with chilies and cumin, undrained
1 can (12 oz.) lager-style beer
1 tablespoon hot pepper sauce
1 teaspoon ground cumin
1 teaspoon ground coriander
½ teaspoon chili powder
½ teaspoon paprika

TOPPINGS (optional):
Sour cream
Shredded Cheddar cheese
Sliced green onions
Snipped fresh cilantro leaves

8 servings

In 6-quart Dutch oven or stockpot, heat 1 tablespoon oil over medium heat. Add venison. Cook for 5 to 7 minutes, or until meat is no longer pink, stirring occasionally. Drain. Remove venison from pot; set aside.

In same pot, heat remaining 1 tablespoon oil over medium heat. Add onion, pepper and garlic. Cook for 3 to 4 minutes, or until onion is tender, stirring occasionally. Stir in venison and remaining ingredients, except toppings. Bring to a boil over high heat, stirring occasionally. Cover. Reduce heat to low. Simmer for 50 to 60 minutes, or until venison is tender and chili is thickened, stirring occasionally. Serve chili with desired toppings.

Per Serving: Calories: 343 • Protein: 41 g.
• Carbohydrate: 28 g. • Fat: 7 g.
• Cholesterol: 119 mg. • Sodium: 526 mg.
Exchanges: 1½ starch, 4 very lean meat, 1¼ vegetable, 1¼ fat

Venison-Vegetable Soup 🔵 LOW-FAT ↑

2 cups beef or venison stock
1 large onion, chopped (1½ cups)
8 oz. red potatoes, chopped (1½ cups)
2 medium carrots, chopped (1 cup)
1 cup shredded white cabbage
2 cloves garlic, minced
8 oz. venison chuck roast, cut into ¼-inch cubes
1 can (14½ oz.) diced tomatoes, undrained
½ teaspoon pepper
½ teaspoon Worcestershire sauce
1 cup fresh or frozen cut green beans
1 cup fresh or frozen corn kernels

8 to 10 servings

In 8-quart stockpot, combine stock, onion, potatoes, carrots, cabbage and garlic. Bring to a boil over high heat. Reduce heat to medium-low. Simmer for 10 to 12 minutes, or until vegetables are tender-crisp.

Meanwhile, spray 10-inch nonstick skillet with nonstick vegetable cooking spray. Add venison. Cook over medium heat for 3 to 5 minutes, or until meat is no longer pink, stirring occasionally. Drain.

Stir venison, tomatoes, pepper and Worcestershire sauce into stockpot. Simmer for 1 hour. Stir in beans and corn. Simmer for 15 to 20 minutes, or until beans and corn are tender, stirring occasionally.

Per Serving: Calories: 89 • Protein: 7 g. • Carbohydrate: 14 g. • Fat: 1 g.
• Cholesterol: 19 mg. • Sodium: 342 mg.
Exchanges: ½ starch, ½ very lean meat, 1¼ vegetable

Dark Beer-Turnip Soup 🏷️

1 lb. venison top round roast, cut
   into 1-inch cubes
1 teaspoon seasoned salt
½ teaspoon freshly ground
   pepper
1 tablespoon vegetable oil
3 tablespoons butter or margarine
1 large onion, chopped (1½ cups)
2 medium carrots, sliced (1 cup)
2 stalks celery, sliced (1 cup)
¼ cup all-purpose flour
4 cups beef or venison stock
2 bottles (12 oz. each) dark,
   German-style beer
8 oz. fresh mushrooms, quartered
3 to 4 medium turnips, peeled
   and chopped (2 cups)
1 teaspoon packed brown sugar
½ teaspoon ground allspice
1 bay leaf
1 tablespoon Worcestershire
   sauce
   Salt to taste

6 to 8 servings

Sprinkle venison cubes evenly with
seasoned salt and pepper. In 6-quart
Dutch oven or stockpot, heat oil
over medium heat. Add venison.
Cook for 4 to 6 minutes, or until
meat is no longer pink, stirring
occasionally. Remove venison
from pot; set aside. Wipe out pot.

In same pot, melt butter over medium heat. Add onion, carrots and
celery. Cook for 5 to 7 minutes, or
until vegetables are tender, stirring
occasionally. Stir in flour. Cook for
1 minute, stirring constantly. Blend
in stock and beer. Stir in remaining
ingredients, except Worcestershire
sauce and salt. Bring to a boil over
high heat. Reduce heat to medium.
Simmer for 25 to 35 minutes, or
until vegetables are tender, stirring
occasionally. Stir in Worcestershire
and salt to taste. Remove and discard bay leaf.

Per Serving: Calories: 200 • Protein: 16 g.
• Carbohydrate: 16 g. • Fat: 8 g.
• Cholesterol: 59 mg. • Sodium: 702 mg.
Exchanges: ¼ starch, 1½ very lean meat,
1½ vegetable, 1¾ fat

Slow-cooking Oven Venison Stew 🏷️ ↑

*This hearty stew is very easy to throw together, then put in the oven and forget about until
dinnertime. It's perfect when you are entertaining a large crowd.*

4 cups beef or venison stock
1½ lbs. venison chuck roast, cut
   into 1-inch cubes
1 can (28 oz.) diced tomatoes,
   undrained
1 lb. red potatoes, quartered
1 lb. baby carrots
1 pkg. (16 oz.) frozen small
   white onions
1 pkg. (10 oz.) frozen cut
   green beans

4 stalks celery, cut into 1-inch
   pieces (2 cups)
2 tablespoons quick-cooking
   tapioca
1 clove garlic, minced
1 teaspoon dried thyme leaves
½ teaspoon pepper
½ teaspoon salt
1 bay leaf

8 to 10 servings

Heat oven to 325°F. In 6-quart Dutch oven or roasting pan, combine all
ingredients. Cover. Bake for 4 to 4½ hours, or until vegetables are tender,
stirring occasionally. Remove and discard bay leaf.

Per Serving: Calories: 196 • Protein: 19 g. • Carbohydrate: 25 g. • Fat: 2 g.
• Cholesterol: 58 mg. • Sodium: 614 mg.
Exchanges: ½ starch, 1½ very lean meat, 3½ vegetable, ½ fat

Calico Bean & Venison Sausage Soup

4 quarts water, divided
2 cups mixed dried beans (navy
    beans, lima beans, pinto beans,
    green split peas, red kidney
    beans)
1 lb. venison summer sausage, cut
    into ¾-inch cubes
1 medium onion, chopped (1 cup)
2 stalks celery, sliced (1 cup)
2 medium carrots, chopped (1 cup)
2 tablespoons instant chicken
    bouillon granules
2 cloves garlic, minced
1 teaspoon dried summer savory
    leaves
1 teaspoon dried thyme leaves

SPICE POUCH*:
1 bay leaf
6 whole peppercorns
5 whole cloves

6 to 8 servings

In 8-quart stockpot, combine 2 quarts water and the beans. Bring to a boil over high heat. Boil for 2 minutes, skimming off any foam that forms. Cover. Remove from heat. Let stand for 1 hour. Rinse and drain beans. Return beans to pot. Set aside.

In 12-inch nonstick skillet, cook venison over medium heat for 5 to 7 minutes, or until browned, stirring occasionally. Drain.

Add venison, remaining 2 quarts water and remaining ingredients to pot. Bring to a boil over high heat. Reduce heat to low. Cover. Simmer for 1½ to 2 hours, or until beans are tender, stirring occasionally. Remove and discard spice pouch before serving.

*To make spice pouch, gather spices up in small square of cheesecloth and tie with kitchen string.

Nutritional information not available due to summer sausage.

Italian Meatball Soup →

MEATBALLS:

1½ lbs. lean ground venison, crumbled

⅔ cup seasoned dry bread crumbs

⅓ cup finely chopped onion

¼ cup grated Parmesan cheese

1 egg, slightly beaten

¼ teaspoon salt

¼ teaspoon pepper

1 jar (28 oz.) prepared marinara sauce

3 cups water

1 can (14½ oz.) diced tomatoes, undrained

8 oz. fresh mushrooms, quartered

1 cup frozen cut green beans

3 cloves garlic, minced

1 teaspoon dried Italian seasoning

8 oz. uncooked bowtie pasta

8 to 10 servings

In large mixing bowl, combine all meatball ingredients. Form meatballs into 1-inch balls (about 45 meatballs). Heat 6-quart Dutch oven or stockpot over medium heat. Add meatballs. Cook for 5 to 7 minutes, or until browned, turning meatballs occasionally. (Brown meatballs in batches, if necessary.) Drain.

Stir in remaining ingredients, except pasta. Bring to a boil over high heat. Cover. Reduce heat to medium-low. Simmer for 10 minutes. Stir in pasta. Re-cover. Simmer for 15 to 20 minutes, or until pasta is tender. Garnish individual servings with shredded fresh Parmesan cheese, if desired.

Per Serving: Calories: 364 • Protein: 21 g. • Carbohydrate: 35 g. • Fat: 16 g. • Cholesterol: 81 mg. • Sodium: 908 mg. Exchanges: 1½ starch, 1¾ medium-fat meat, 2½ vegetable, 1½ fat

Mexicali Venison Stew LOW-FAT

This thick, spicy stew can be served in a bowl, or it can be simmered until very thick and used as a tortilla filling topped with sour cream, salsa and cheese.

1 lb. venison top round, cut into ½-inch cubes

1 medium onion, chopped (1 cup)

1 medium green pepper, seeded and chopped (1 cup)

1 jalapeño pepper, seeded and finely chopped

3 cloves garlic, minced

1 can (14½ oz.) diced tomatoes, undrained

1 can (10 oz.) diced tomatoes with chilies, undrained

2 medium tomatillos*, chopped (½ cup)

2 tablespoons golden tequila (optional)

1 tablespoon snipped fresh cilantro

½ teaspoon ground cumin

½ teaspoon dried oregano leaves

¼ teaspoon pepper

1 cup frozen corn kernels

4 to 6 servings

Heat 12-inch nonstick skillet over medium-high heat. Add venison. Cook for 4 to 6 minutes, or until meat is no longer pink, stirring occasionally. With slotted spoon, remove meat from skillet; set aside. Wipe out skillet.

Spray skillet with nonstick vegetable cooking spray. Heat skillet over medium heat. Add onion, green pepper, jalapeño and garlic. Cook for 3 to 4 minutes, or until vegetables are tender-crisp, stirring occasionally. Stir in venison and remaining ingredients, except corn. Bring to a boil. Reduce heat to medium-low. Cover. Simmer for 20 to 25 minutes, or until meat is tender and flavors are blended, stirring occasionally. Stir in corn. Cook, uncovered, for 5 to 6 minutes, or until heated through, stirring occasionally.

Tomatillos belong to the tomato family, but are also related to the cape gooseberry, as their papery husk indicates. Their flavor is a combination of lemon, apple and herbs. Buy firm tomatillos with tight-fitting husks, and remove the husk and wash the fruit before using.

Per Serving: Calories: 162 • Protein: 20 g. • Carbohydrate: 16 g. • Fat: 3 g. • Cholesterol: 64 mg. • Sodium: 335 mg. Exchanges: ¼ starch, 1½ very lean meat, 2¼ vegetable, ½ fat

Ginger Chili 🌶 LOW-FAT

¼ cup dry sherry
2 tablespoons soy sauce
1 lb. venison chuck roast, cut into
   1½ × ½ × ¼-inch strips
2 teaspoons vegetable oil, divided
1 medium onion, chopped (1 cup)
2 jalapeño peppers, seeded and
   finely chopped
1 tablespoon grated fresh
   gingerroot

3 cloves garlic, minced
1 can (28 oz.) diced tomatoes,
   undrained
1 can (8 oz.) tomato sauce
1 tablespoon chili powder
½ teaspoon sugar
½ teaspoon salt
½ teaspoon pepper

4 servings

In large, sealable food-storage bag, combine sherry and soy sauce. Add venison, seal bag and turn to coat. Refrigerate 1 hour.

Meanwhile, in 3-quart saucepan, heat 1 teaspoon oil over medium heat. Add onion, jalapeños, gingerroot and garlic. Cook for 3 to 5 minutes, or until vegetables are tender, stirring occasionally. Stir in tomatoes, tomato sauce, chili powder, sugar, salt and pepper. Bring to a boil over high heat. Reduce heat to low. Simmer for 1 hour.

Drain and discard marinade from venison. In 10-inch nonstick skillet, heat remaining 1 teaspoon oil over medium heat. Add venison. Cook for 3 to 5 minutes, or until no longer pink, stirring occasionally. Drain. Stir venison into saucepan.

Serve chili with sour cream, sliced green onions and shredded cheese, if desired.

TIP: If desired, add ½ cup chopped red pepper and/or 1 can of rinsed and drained kidney beans to chili. Add red pepper with onion; add beans with tomatoes.

Per Serving: Calories: 246 • Protein: 30 g. • Carbohydrate: 20 g. • Fat: 6 g.
• Cholesterol: 95 mg. • Sodium: 1265 mg.
Exchanges: 3 very lean meat, 4 vegetable, 1 fat

← Venison Sausage Tortilla Soup ⬤ VERY FAST

This is a spicy, sassy recipe. For a tamer soup, substitute regular venison sausage for the spicy sausage.

1 lb. spicy bratwurst-style
   venison sausages (see page
   109), coarsely chopped
3 cans (10 oz. each) diced
   tomatoes with chilies,
   undrained
1 can (14½ oz.) ready-to-serve
   chicken broth
1 cup water
1 medium onion, chopped (1 cup)
2 cloves garlic, minced
½ teaspoon ground cumin
¼ teaspoon salt
¼ teaspoon pepper
2 corn tortillas (6-inch), cut into
   thin strips
1 cup shredded Cheddar cheese

4 to 6 servings

In 6-quart Dutch oven or stockpot, cook sausages over medium heat for 5 to 7 minutes, or until browned, stirring occasionally. Drain. Wipe out pot. Return sausages to pot.

Add remaining ingredients, except tortillas and cheese. Bring to a boil over high heat. Reduce heat to medium-low. Simmer for 20 minutes to blend flavors, stirring occasionally. Sprinkle tortilla strips and cheese evenly over individual servings. Garnish with sour cream and snipped fresh cilantro, if desired.

Per Serving: Calories: 337 • Protein: 21 g.
• Carbohydrate: 12 g. • Fat: 23 g.
• Cholesterol: 81 mg. • Sodium: 1364 mg.
Exchanges: ¼ starch, 2¾ medium-fat meat, 1½ vegetable, 1½ fat

Venison Gumbo

Gumbo, a Creole specialty prominent in New Orleans, is a thick, spicy stew that uses vegetables such as okra, tomatoes and onions, and meats such as sausage, chicken or shrimp. The name gumbo is actually from the African word for okra. Our recipe features okra and spicy venison sausage as the stars.

1 lb. spicy bratwurst-style venison sausages (see page 109), sliced
2 tablespoons butter or margarine
1 cup sliced green onions
1 green pepper, seeded and chopped (1 cup)
½ cup snipped fresh parsley
2 cloves garlic, minced
1 pkg. (16 oz.) frozen cut okra
1 can (16 oz.) stewed tomatoes, cut up
1 can (15 oz.) tomato sauce
1 can (10¾ oz.) condensed chicken broth
1 teaspoon Worcestershire sauce
½ teaspoon dried thyme leaves
½ teaspoon dried oregano leaves
½ teaspoon dried basil leaves
⅛ to ¼ teaspoon cayenne
1 bay leaf
 Hot cooked white rice (optional)

6 servings

In 6-quart Dutch oven or stockpot, cook sausages over medium heat for 5 to 7 minutes, or until browned, stirring occasionally. Drain. Set sausages aside on paper-towel-lined plate. Wipe out pot.

In same pot, melt butter over medium heat. Add onions, green pepper, parsley and garlic. Cook for 5 to 7 minutes, or until vegetables are tender, stirring occasionally. Stir in remaining ingredients, except rice. Bring to a boil over high heat, stirring occasionally. Reduce heat to medium-low. Simmer for 15 to 20 minutes, or until okra is tender, stirring occasionally. Remove and discard bay leaf. Serve gumbo over rice.

Per Serving: Calories: 488 • Protein: 27 g. • Carbohydrate: 29 g. • Fat: 31 g. • Cholesterol: 109 mg. • Sodium: 1931 mg. Exchanges: 3 medium-fat meat, 5½ vegetable, 3¼ fat

Wonton Soup

FILLING:

8 oz. lean ground venison, crumbled

¼ cup sliced green onions (white part only)

2 tablespoons sliced water chestnuts

1 tablespoon soy sauce

1 teaspoon cornstarch

1 teaspoon dry sherry

½ teaspoon ground ginger

40 wonton skins

8 cups water

8 cups ready-to-serve chicken broth*

1 can (8 oz.) sliced bamboo shoots

¾ cup sliced water chestnuts

1 oz. dried shiitake mushrooms, soaked** and sliced, or 4 oz. fresh shiitake mushrooms, sliced

1 cup cut green onion tops, 2-inch lengths

¼ teaspoon white pepper

8 servings

Per Serving: Calories: 255 • Protein: 12 g.
• Carbohydrate: 31 g. • Fat: 8 g.
• Cholesterol: 29 mg. • Sodium: 1374 mg.
Exchanges: 1½ starch, ¾ high-fat meat, 1½ vegetable, ½ fat

On cutting board, chop venison, onions and 2 tablespoons water chestnuts until finely chopped. In medium mixing bowl, combine meat mixture and remaining filling ingredients. Follow photo directions for making wontons.

In 6-quart Dutch oven or stockpot, bring water to a boil over high heat. Add wontons, stirring gently to prevent them from sticking to bottom of pot. (You may have to cook wontons in batches.) Cook for 3 minutes. Remove wontons from pot. Rinse wontons with cold water and drain. Set aside.

In same pot, bring broth to a boil over high heat. Stir in bamboo shoots, water chestnuts and mushrooms. Reduce heat to medium. Simmer for 5 minutes. Stir in wontons, onion tops and pepper. Simmer for 2 to 3 minutes, or until heated through.

*If you wish to reduce the sodium level of this recipe, use reduced-sodium chicken broth, or substitute water for part of the chicken broth.

**To soak dried mushrooms, cover them with boiling water and let stand for 30 minutes; drain. Remove any tough stems before slicing.

How to Fold Wontons

PLACE rounded teaspoon filling in center of wonton skin. Moisten edges of wonton with water. Fold wonton skin diagonally over filling, pressing edges to seal.

MOISTEN one corner of wonton. Bring two corners together and overlap. Press together to seal. Repeat with remaining filling and wonton skins.

74

Venison Ragout LOW-FAT

2 tablespoons vegetable oil
2 medium onions, coarsely
   chopped (2 cups)
2 lbs. venison chuck roast, cut
   into ½-inch cubes
3 cans (12 oz. each) lager-style
   beer, room temperature
4 cups water, beef stock or
   venison stock
2 tablespoons sweet Hungarian
   paprika
1 clove garlic, minced
1 teaspoon caraway seed
1 teaspoon salt
½ teaspoon pepper
3 medium tomatoes, peeled,
   seeded and coarsely chopped
   (3 cups)
1 lb. russet potatoes, peeled and
   cut into ¼-inch cubes
   (2½ cups)
2 teaspoons hot pepper sauce
⅓ cup snipped fresh parsley

8 servings

In 8-quart stockpot, heat oil over
medium-high heat. Add onions.
Cook for 4 to 6 minutes, or until
tender, stirring occasionally. Add
venison. Cook for 3 to 5 minutes,
or until meat is no longer pink,
stirring occasionally.

Stir in beer, water, paprika, garlic,
caraway seed, salt and pepper. Bring
to a boil over medium-high heat,
stirring occasionally. Reduce heat
to medium. Simmer for 1 hour. Stir
in tomatoes, potatoes and pepper
sauce. Simmer for 20 to 25 minutes,
or until potatoes are tender, stirring
occasionally. Stir in parsley just
before serving.

Per Serving: Calories: 266 • Protein: 29 g.
• Carbohydrate: 22 g. • Fat: 7 g.
• Cholesterol: 96 mg. • Sodium: 385 mg.
Exchanges: ½ starch, 3 very lean meat,
1½ vegetable, 1¼ fat

Hungarian-style Goulash ↑

1½ lbs. lean ground venison,
   crumbled
4 teaspoons sweet Hungarian
   paprika, divided
3 tablespoons vegetable oil
1 medium onion, coarsely
   chopped (1¼ cups)
2 stalks celery, cut into ½-inch
   slices (1 cup)
3 cloves garlic, crushed
¼ cup all-purpose flour
1 can (28 oz.) whole tomatoes,
   undrained and coarsely
   chopped

2 cups beef or venison stock
1 can (15 oz.) tomato sauce
8 oz. fresh mushrooms, sliced
   (3 cups)
1 lb. russet potatoes, peeled
   and cut into ½-inch cubes
   (2½ cups)
1 tablespoon Worcestershire
   sauce
1 teaspoon coarsely ground
   pepper
Sour cream (optional)

8 servings

In large mixing bowl, combine venison and 2 teaspoons paprika. Drop
mixture by heaping teaspoons into 6-quart Dutch oven or stockpot. Cook
over medium heat for 6 to 8 minutes, or until pieces are browned, stirring
occasionally. Using slotted spoon, place pieces on paper-towel-lined plate.
Drain and wipe out skillet.

In same skillet, heat oil over medium heat. Add onion, celery and garlic.
Cook for 5 to 7 minutes, or until vegetables are tender-crisp, stirring occasionally. Stir in flour. Cook for 2 minutes, stirring constantly.

Blend in tomatoes, stock and tomato sauce. Stir in venison and remaining
2 teaspoons paprika. Simmer for 20 minutes to blend flavors, stirring
occasionally. Stir in mushrooms, potatoes, Worcestershire sauce and pepper.
Simmer for 20 to 25 minutes, or until potatoes are tender, stirring occasionally. Garnish individual servings with dollop of sour cream, if desired.

Per Serving: Calories: 342 • Protein: 21 g. • Carbohydrate: 26 g. • Fat: 18 g.
• Cholesterol: 70 mg. • Sodium: 738 mg.
Exchanges: ¾ starch, 2 lean meat, 3 vegetable, 2¼ fat

New Mexican-style Red Chili

New Mexican chili is not your typical chili. It has very few ingredients and relies on roasted dried chili peppers to create a rich, gravy-like sauce. The flavor and "hotness" of the dish can vary, depending on the dried chilies you choose.

1 oz. dried ancho chilies
1 oz. dried New Mexican red
    chilies, or other dried red
    chilies
1 small onion, coarsely chopped
    (3/4 cup)
4 to 6 whole cloves garlic
4 cups water, divided
1 1/2 lbs. venison top round steak,
    cut into 1/2-inch cubes
1 teaspoon salt

4 servings

Per Serving: Calories: 255 • Protein: 41 g.
• Carbohydrate: 10 g. • Fat: 6 g.
• Cholesterol: 145 mg. • Sodium: 642 mg.
Exchanges: 4 1/2 very lean meat,
2 vegetable, 1 fat

Heat oven to 400°F. Remove and discard stems from chilies. If desired, remove and discard seeds*. Rinse chilies with cold water, and arrange them in single layer on large baking sheet. Roast for 5 minutes. (Do not burn.)

Coarsely chop chilies. In blender or food processor, combine chilies, onion, garlic and 1/2 cup water. Process until finely chopped. Transfer mixture to 4-quart saucepan. Add remaining 3 1/2 cups water. Add venison.

Bring to a boil over medium-high heat. Cover. Reduce heat to low. Simmer for 30 minutes. Uncover. Simmer for 30 to 40 minutes longer, or until chili is desired thickness, stirring occasionally. Stir in salt. Serve chili with tortilla chips or over corn bread, if desired.

The seeds hold most of a chili pepper's heat. Remove them for a milder chili.

TIP: Serve chili as a sauce over cheese-filled tortillas, if desired.

Venison Sausage Jambalaya →

1½ lbs. spicy bratwurst-style
    venison sausages (see page
    109), sliced
  3 stalks celery, cut into ½-inch
    slices (1½ cups)
  1 medium onion, chopped
    (1 cup)
  1 medium green pepper, seeded
    and chopped (1 cup)
  2 cloves garlic, minced
  1 tablespoon Cajun seasoning
  1 bay leaf
  1 can (28 oz.) diced tomatoes,
    undrained
  2 cups water
  1 can (15 oz.) tomato sauce
  2 cups uncooked converted
    white rice
 ½ cup sliced green onions

8 servings

In 6-quart Dutch oven or stockpot,
cook sausages, celery, chopped
onion, pepper and garlic over
medium heat for 10 to 12 minutes,
or until meat is browned and vegetables are tender, stirring occasionally. Drain. Return to heat.

Stir in Cajun seasoning and bay
leaf. Cook for 2 minutes, stirring
constantly. Blend in tomatoes,
water and tomato sauce. Bring to
a boil over medium-high heat. Stir
in rice and green onions. Return to
a boil. Cover. Reduce heat to low.
Simmer for 15 to 20 minutes, or
until rice is nearly tender. Remove
from heat. Let stand, covered, for
5 minutes. Remove and discard
bay leaf.

Per Serving: Calories: 454 • Protein: 21 g.
• Carbohydrate: 51 g. • Fat: 18 g.
• Cholesterol: 69 mg. • Sodium: 1141 mg.
Exchanges: 2¾ starch, 2 medium-fat meat,
2 vegetable, 1¼ fat

Wild Rice Soup ●VERY FAST

  1 lb. lean ground venison,
    crumbled
 ½ cup butter or margarine
 ¼ cup finely chopped onion
 ¾ cup all-purpose flour
  6 cups ready-to-serve chicken
    broth
  4 cups cooked wild rice

  1 cup shredded carrots
 ⅓ cup slivered almonds
  1 to 2 teaspoons seasoned salt
  1 teaspoon freshly ground
    pepper
1½ cups 2% milk
 ¼ cup dry sherry (optional)

8 servings

In 6-quart Dutch oven or stockpot, cook venison over medium heat for 6
to 8 minutes, or until meat is no longer pink, stirring occasionally. Drain.
Remove meat from pot. Set aside. Wipe out pot.

In same pot, melt butter over medium heat. Add onion. Cook for 2 to 3
minutes, or until tender, stirring occasionally. Stir in flour. Cook for 1
minute, stirring constantly. Gradually whisk in broth. Cook for 6 to 8 minutes, or until soup comes to a boil, stirring constantly. Cook for 1 minute,
stirring constantly.

Stir in venison, rice, carrots, almonds, salt and pepper. Simmer for 5 minutes, stirring occasionally. Stir in milk and sherry. Cook for 4 to 6 minutes,
or until heated through, stirring occasionally. (Do not boil.) Garnish soup
with snipped fresh parsley or chives, if desired.

Per Serving: Calories: 431 • Protein: 20 g. • Carbohydrate: 32 g. • Fat: 25 g.
• Cholesterol: 82 mg. • Sodium: 1159 mg.
Exchanges: 1¾ starch, 1½ medium-fat meat, ¼ vegetable, ¼ low-fat milk, 3¼ fat

Appetizers & Small Meals

Appetizers

← Venison-stuffed Portobello Mushrooms ⬤ VERY FAST

This recipe makes an elegant and flavorful meal-starter for a small dinner party.

6 medium portobello mushrooms
  (4-inch diameter)
½ lb. lean ground venison,
  crumbled
1 clove garlic, minced
½ cup finely chopped red pepper
1 tablespoon snipped fresh parsley
1 teaspoon fresh thyme leaves
1 teaspoon salt
¼ teaspoon crushed red pepper
  flakes
¼ teaspoon freshly ground black
  pepper
2 tablespoons olive oil

6 servings

Heat oven to 450°F. Position oven rack in top third of oven. Cut stems off mushrooms flush with cap. Arrange caps on baking sheet, top-side-down. Set aside. Finely chop stems. Set aside.

In 10-inch nonstick skillet, cook venison over medium heat for 5 to 6 minutes, or until meat is no longer pink. Drain. Stir in garlic and chopped mushroom stems. Cook for 3 to 5 minutes, or until stems begin to release liquid, stirring occasionally. Stir in remaining ingredients, except oil.

Spoon mixture evenly into mushroom caps. Drizzle oil evenly over filling in caps. Bake for 10 to 15 minutes, or until mushrooms are soft.

If desired, sprinkle shredded fresh Parmesan cheese over mushrooms during last few minutes of baking.

TIP: Portobello mushrooms are very large, meaty mushrooms with a rich, earthy flavor.

Per Serving: Calories: 150 • Protein: 10 g. • Carbohydrate: 6 g. • Fat: 10 g.
• Cholesterol: 31 mg. • Sodium: 388 mg.
Exchanges: 1 medium-fat meat, 1¼ vegetable, 1 fat

Grilled Venison Quesadillas ⬤ FAST

MARINADE:
3 tablespoons olive oil
2 tablespoons lime juice
2 teaspoons chili powder
1 clove garlic, minced
½ teaspoon ground cumin
¼ teaspoon salt
¼ teaspoon pepper

½-lb. venison loin steak, ½ to
  ¾ inch thick
4 whole fresh jalapeño peppers
8 flour tortillas (6-inch)
2 cups shredded Monterey Jack
  cheese, divided
  Fresh cilantro sprigs (optional)

8 servings

Combine marinade ingredients in large sealable plastic bag. Add venison, seal bag and turn to coat. Refrigerate 30 minutes, turning bag once or twice.

Prepare grill for medium direct heat. Grill jalapeño peppers for 10 to 12 minutes, or until blackened on all sides, turning peppers occasionally. Place peppers in paper bag. Let steam for 10 minutes. Peel peppers, and remove seeds, if desired. Cut peppers into thin strips. Set aside.

Drain and discard marinade from meat. Grill steak for 6 to 8 minutes, or until meat is desired doneness, turning steak over once. Thinly slice meat across grain.

Arrange 4 tortillas on grill. Top tortillas evenly with 1 cup cheese, then venison slices, peppers and cilantro sprigs. Sprinkle remaining 1 cup cheese evenly over top, and top with remaining 4 tortillas. Grill for 3 to 4 minutes, or until tortillas are golden and cheese is melted, turning quesadillas over once. Cut quesadillas into wedges to serve.

Per Serving: Calories: 231 • Protein: 15 g. • Carbohydrate: 12 g. • Fat: 13 g.
• Cholesterol: 54 mg. • Sodium: 298 mg.
Exchanges: 1 starch, 1¾ very lean meat, 2½ fat

4 lbs. venison ribs*, cut apart

SAUCE:
2 tablespoons olive oil
1 medium onion, chopped (1 cup)
1 clove garlic, minced
1 cup honey
1 can (6 oz.) tomato paste
1 can (6 oz.) pineapple juice
2 tablespoons hot pepper sauce
2 tablespoons molasses
1 teaspoon ground cumin
1 teaspoon salt
1 teaspoon black pepper

8 servings

Heat oven to 375°F. Arrange ribs in single layer on large baking sheet with edges. Set aside.

In 2-quart saucepan, heat oil over medium heat. Add onion and garlic. Cook for 8 to 10 minutes, or until onion begins to turn golden, stirring occasionally. Whisk in remaining sauce ingredients. Bring to a boil over medium-high heat. Reduce heat to medium-low. Simmer for 10 to 15 minutes, or until sauce is slightly thickened, stirring occasionally.

Pour sauce over ribs, turning ribs to coat. Cover with foil. Bake for 30 minutes. Remove foil. Bake for 30 to 45 minutes longer, or until liquid begins to thicken and meat is tender, basting ribs occasionally.

*Leave an extra outer layer of meat or a portion of the loin attached to ribs when butchering.

Per Serving: Calories: 414 • Protein: 40 g.
• Carbohydrate: 48 g. • Fat: 8 g.
• Cholesterol: 143 mg. • Sodium: 615 mg.
Exchanges: 4½ very lean meat,
1 vegetable, 1½ fat

Spicy Chinese Venison Ribs

4 lbs. venison ribs*, cut apart
2/3 cup hoisin sauce
1 can (6 oz.) tomato paste
1/3 cup sugar

1/4 cup rice vinegar
6 cloves garlic, minced
1 teaspoon hot pepper sauce

8 servings

Heat oven to 375°F. Arrange ribs in single layer on large baking sheet with edges. Set aside.

In medium mixing bowl, combine remaining ingredients. Pour mixture over ribs, turning ribs to coat. Cover with foil. Bake for 30 minutes. Remove foil. Bake for 30 to 45 minutes longer, or until liquid begins to thicken and meat is tender, basting ribs occasionally.

*Leave an extra outer layer of meat or a portion of the loin attached to ribs when butchering.

TIP: Hoisin sauce is a thick, sweet and spicy sauce used in Chinese cooking. It is made from soybeans, garlic, chili peppers and various spices.

Per Serving: Calories: 316 • Protein: 39 g. • Carbohydrate: 25 g. • Fat: 4 g.
• Cholesterol: 143 mg. • Sodium: 676 mg.
Exchanges: 4½ very lean meat, 1 fat

Barbecued Venison Nachos ●FAST

1 can (16 oz.) fat-free refried
   black beans
1½ cups shredded Cheddar
   cheese, divided
½ cup barbecue sauce
½ lb. lean ground venison,
   crumbled
1 small onion, chopped
   (½ cup)
½ cup red or green salsa

GARNISHES (optional):
   Sliced black olives
   Chopped seeded tomato
   Chopped avocado
   Sliced green onions
   Sliced jalapeño peppers

6 to 8 servings

Heat oven to 350°F. In medium mixing bowl, combine beans, 1 cup cheese and the barbecue sauce. Set aside.

In 8-inch nonstick skillet, cook venison and onion over medium heat for 5 to 6 minutes, or until onion is tender and meat is no longer pink, stirring occasionally. Drain. Stir meat mixture into bean mixture. Spread mixture on ovenproof platter or in deep, 10-inch pie plate. Top evenly with salsa.

Bake dip for 15 to 25 minutes*, or until heated through and bean mixture darkens. Top with remaining ½ cup cheese and desired garnishes. Serve with tortilla chips.

*Baking time will be shorter if using a platter and longer if using a pie plate.

Per Serving: Calories: 210 • Protein: 14 g. • Carbohydrate: 13 g. • Fat: 11 g.
• Cholesterol: 46 mg. • Sodium: 611 mg.
Exchanges: ½ starch, 1½ medium-fat meat, 1 vegetable, ¾ fat

Venison Meatballs in Wine Sauce

MEATBALLS:

1 lb. lean ground venison, crumbled
4 oz. ground pork, crumbled
½ cup unseasoned dry bread crumbs
¼ cup dry red wine
1 egg, slightly beaten
2 cloves garlic, minced
2 teaspoons oregano
1 teaspoon hot pepper sauce
1 teaspoon Worcestershire sauce
1 teaspoon salt
½ teaspoon pepper

SAUCE:

1 cup beef or venison stock
½ cup dry red wine
2 tablespoons Dijon mustard
1 tablespoon tomato paste
1 tablespoon Worcestershire sauce
1 teaspoon dried oregano leaves
½ teaspoon salt
½ teaspoon pepper

10 to 12 servings

Heat oven to 450°F. In large mixing bowl, combine meatball ingredients. Shape mixture into 40 meatballs, about 1½ inches in diameter. Arrange meatballs in single layer in 13 × 9-inch baking pan. Bake for 20 to 25 minutes, or until meatballs are firm and no longer pink, turning meatballs over once. Drain.

Meanwhile, in 1-quart saucepan, combine sauce ingredients. Bring to a boil over medium-high heat. Reduce heat to medium-low. Simmer for 7 to 8 minutes, or until sauce is slightly thickened, stirring occasionally.

Arrange meatballs in serving dish. Pour sauce over meatballs, tossing lightly to coat.

Per Serving: Calories: 164 • Protein: 10 g.
• Carbohydrate: 5 g. • Fat: 10 g.
• Cholesterol: 58 mg. • Sodium: 509 mg.
Exchanges: ⅓ starch, 1¼ medium-fat meat, ¾ fat

Venison Satay with Spicy Peanut Sauce ● VERY FAST →

Satay is an Indonesian favorite consisting of marinated meat threaded on skewers, grilled or broiled, and served with a spicy peanut sauce for dipping.

1 lb. venison loin steaks, well trimmed, cut into 4 × ½ × ¼-inch strips
¼ cup rice vinegar
¼ cup soy sauce
12 wooden skewers (6-inch)

PEANUT SAUCE:

⅓ cup chunky peanut butter
2 tablespoons water
2 tablespoons soy sauce
2 tablespoons rice vinegar
2 cloves garlic, minced
2 teaspoons grated fresh gingerroot
1 teaspoon sugar
¼ teaspoon crushed red pepper flakes
¼ teaspoon hot pepper sauce (optional)

6 servings

In shallow dish, combine venison strips, vinegar and soy sauce. Cover with plastic wrap. Refrigerate 30 minutes. Soak skewers in warm water for 30 minutes. Drain.

In small mixing bowl, combine sauce ingredients. Set aside.

Drain and discard marinade from meat strips. Evenly thread strips, accordion-style, on skewers. Spray rack in broiler pan with nonstick vegetable cooking spray. Arrange skewers on prepared rack. Place skewers under broiler with surface of meat 4 to 5 inches from heat. Broil for 4 to 5 minutes, or until meat is no longer pink, turning skewers over once. Serve skewers hot with peanut sauce.

Per Serving: Calories: 183 • Protein: 21 g. • Carbohydrate: 5 g. • Fat: 9 g.
• Cholesterol: 63 mg. • Sodium: 614 mg.
Exchanges: 2¾ very lean meat, 1¾ fat

Stuffed Crimini Mushrooms ● VERY FAST →

This is a very easy stuffed mushroom recipe. The mushrooms can be stuffed up to 4 hours ahead of time, then covered and refrigerated until ready to bake.

42 fresh medium crimini mushrooms (1 lb.)
½ cup pine nuts
½ lb. venison summer sausage, finely chopped (2 cups)
1 container (6 oz.) prepared pesto

14 servings

Preheat oven to 400°F. Remove stems from mushroom caps. Discard stems or reserve for other uses. Arrange caps top-side-down on large baking sheet with edges. Set aside.

In 8-inch skillet, toast pine nuts over medium heat for 6 to 8 minutes, or until lightly browned, shaking pan frequently. Place in medium mixing bowl. Stir in sausage and pesto. Spoon sausage mixture evenly into mushroom caps. Bake for 6 to 8 minutes, or until mushrooms are soft.

TIP: Crimini mushrooms are brown Italian mushrooms, similar in size to white, cultivated mushrooms.

Nutritional information not available due to summer sausage.

Herbed Venison Empanadas ●FAST ↑

FILLING:

½ lb. lean ground venison,
    crumbled
1 medium onion, chopped (1 cup)
1 tablespoon paprika
2 teaspoons dried oregano leaves
1 teaspoon sugar

½ teaspoon salt
½ teaspoon black pepper
½ cup crumbled feta cheese

1 package (11 oz.) pie crust mix
1 egg, lightly beaten

20 empanadas

In 12-inch nonstick skillet, cook venison and onion over medium-high
heat for 10 to 12 minutes, or until venison is no longer pink and onion is
tender, stirring occasionally. Drain. Stir in remaining filling ingredients,
except feta. Transfer filling to large mixing bowl. Cover and chill. Stir in
feta when filling is cool.

Heat oven to 375°F. Prepare crust as directed on package. Pinch off
enough dough to form 1 to 1½-inch ball. On lightly floured surface, roll
ball into 4-inch circle. Place heaping tablespoon filling in center of circle.
Brush edges of circle lightly with water. Fold circle in half over filling,
pressing edges with tines of fork to seal. Place empanada on parchment-
lined baking sheet. Repeat with remaining dough and filling.

Brush empanadas with beaten egg. Bake for 30 to 35 minutes, or until
empanadas are golden brown. Serve hot.

TIP: You may substitute your favorite two-crust pie crust recipe for pack-
aged mix.

Per Serving: Calories: 130 • Protein: 4 g. • Carbohydrate: 9 g. • Fat: 9 g.
• Cholesterol: 23 mg. • Sodium: 221 mg.
Exchanges: ½ starch, ½ medium-fat meat, 1¼ fat

Grilled Pizzas with Venison Sausage, Brie & Pesto

CRUST:

1 cup warm water (105° to 115°F)
1 tablespoon quick-rising active
    dry yeast
2 tablespoons olive oil
1 teaspoon salt
3½ cups all-purpose flour

½ lb. venison summer sausage,
    thinly sliced
1 container (6 oz.) prepared
    pesto, divided
8 oz. brie, thinly sliced with rind
    Red pepper flakes (optional)

8 servings

In large mixing bowl, combine
water and yeast. Let stand for 5
minutes, or until bubbly. Stir in oil
and salt. Stir in 2 cups flour. Beat
well. Gradually stir in enough
of remaining flour to form soft
dough that pulls away from sides
of bowl. Turn dough out onto
lightly floured surface. Knead for
8 to 10 minutes, or until smooth
and elastic, adding flour as necessary to prevent stickiness.

Place dough in bowl that has been
sprayed with nonstick vegetable
cooking spray, turning to coat
dough. Cover with light cloth. Let
rise in warm place for 30 to 40
minutes, or until doubled in size.

Prepare grill for medium indirect
heat. Grill sausage slices briefly to
warm them, turning slices over
once. Set aside and keep warm.
Divide dough into 4 equal pieces.
Press each piece into oval. Place
1 or 2 ovals on grill. Grill until
bubbles start to form in dough and
bottom of crust is lightly browned.
Turn crust over. Top each crust
with one-fourth of pesto, sausage
and brie. Sprinkle lightly with red
pepper flakes. Cook for 8 to 10
minutes, or until bottom of crust
is browned and toppings are hot.
Repeat with remaining dough and
toppings. Cut each pizza into 4
wedges to serve.

Nutritional information not available due
to summer sausage.

Sandwiches

Snappy Sloppy Joes ⏵FAST

- 2 lbs. lean ground venison, crumbled
- 8 oz. fresh mushrooms, sliced (3 cups)
- 1 medium onion, chopped (1 cup)
- 1 jar (12 oz.) chili sauce
- 1 cup catsup
- 1/2 cup water
- 1 to 2 tablespoons Worcestershire sauce
- 1 tablespoon fresh horseradish
- 1 teaspoon red pepper sauce
- 1/2 teaspoon garlic powder
- 1/2 teaspoon celery seed
- 1/2 teaspoon salt
- 8 to 10 hamburger buns, split

8 to 10 servings

In 6-quart Dutch oven or stockpot, combine venison, mushrooms and onion. Cook over medium heat for 12 to 15 minutes, or until meat is no longer pink, stirring occasionally. Drain.

Stir in remaining ingredients, except buns. Bring to a simmer. Simmer for 20 to 25 minutes, or until flavors are blended and mixture is desired thickness, stirring occasionally. Serve mixture on buns. Serve with dill pickle and tomato slices, if desired.

Per Serving: Calories: 436 • Protein: 23 g. • Carbohydrate: 40 g. • Fat: 21 g. • Cholesterol: 81 mg. • Sodium: 1169 mg. Exchanges: 2 starch, 2 medium-fat meat, 2 vegetable, 2 fat

Jerked Venison Burgers with Mango Salsa ⏵VERY FAST ↑

MANGO SALSA:
- 2 medium mangos, peeled and chopped (2 cups)
- 1 medium cucumber, peeled, seeded and chopped (1 cup)
- 1/2 cup sliced green onions
- 2 tablespoons snipped fresh cilantro
- 1/2 habañero pepper, seeded and finely chopped
- 1 tablespoon fresh lime juice
- 1 teaspoon sugar
  Dash salt

JERK SEASONING PASTE:
- 2 tablespoons white vinegar
- 1/2 habañero pepper, seeded and finely chopped

- 2 teaspoons fresh thyme leaves
- 1 teaspoon soy sauce
- 1 teaspoon salt
- 1 teaspoon onion powder
- 1 teaspoon garlic powder
- 3/4 teaspoon ground allspice
- 1/2 teaspoon black pepper
- 1/1 teaspoon ground nutmeg
- 1/4 teaspoon ground cinnamon

- 1 1/2 lbs. lean ground venison, crumbled
- 6 hamburger buns, split
  Lettuce leaves

6 servings

In small mixing bowl, combine salsa ingredients. Set aside. In medium mixing bowl, combine seasoning paste. Add venison. Mix well to combine. Shape mixture into six 1/2-inch-thick patties.

Heat 12-inch nonstick skillet over medium heat. Spray skillet with non-stick vegetable cooking spray. Add patties. Cook for 6 to 8 minutes, or until meat is desired doneness, turning patties over once.

Place patties on lettuce-lined buns. Top with salsa.

TIP: Habañero peppers are extremely hot. Wear rubber gloves when handling them, and avoid rubbing your eyes.

Per Serving: Calories: 411 • Protein: 26 g. • Carbohydrate: 35 g. • Fat: 18 g. • Cholesterol: 94 mg. • Sodium: 739 mg. Exchanges: 1 1/2 starch, 3 lean meat, 1 vegetable, 1/2 fruit, 2 fat

Mexican Burgers ● VERY FAST ↑

1 lb. lean ground venison, crumbled	4 hamburger buns, split
1 pkg. (1¼ oz.) taco seasoning mix	4 slices tomato
2 tablespoons cold water	4 lettuce leaves
8 slices (1 oz. each) Cheddar or American cheese	¼ cup salsa
	¼ cup sour cream

4 servings

In medium mixing bowl, combine venison, seasoning mix and water. Shape mixture into four ½-inch-thick patties.

Heat 12-inch nonstick skillet over medium heat. Spray skillet with non-stick vegetable cooking spray. Add patties. Cook for 6 to 8 minutes, or until meat is desired doneness, turning patties over once. Remove from heat. Top each patty with 2 slices cheese.

Place patties in buns with tomato slices, lettuce leaves, salsa and sour cream.

Per Serving: Calories: 659 • Protein: 40 g. • Carbohydrate: 30 g. • Fat: 40 g.
• Cholesterol: 160 mg. • Sodium: 1550 mg.
Exchanges: 1½ starch, 4½ high-fat meat, 1½ vegetable, ¾ fat

Ranch Burgers ● VERY FAST ↑

⅓ cup sour cream
1 tablespoon plus 1 teaspoon ranch dressing mix, divided
1 lb. lean ground venison, crumbled
¼ cup sliced green onions
2 tablespoons cold water
⅛ teaspoon pepper
4 hamburger buns, split

4 servings

In small mixing bowl, combine sour cream and 1 teaspoon dressing mix. Cover with plastic wrap. Chill.

In medium mixing bowl, combine venison, green onions, water, pepper and remaining 1 tablespoon dressing mix. Mix well. Shape mixture into four ½-inch-thick patties.

Heat 12-inch nonstick skillet over medium heat. Spray skillet with nonstick vegetable cooking spray. Add patties. Cook for 6 to 8 minutes, or until meat is desired doneness, turning patties over once. Place patties in buns and top evenly with sour cream mixture.

Per Serving: Calories: 412 • Protein: 26 g. • Carbohydrate: 25 g. • Fat: 22 g. • Cholesterol: 102 mg. • Sodium: 560 mg. Exchanges: 1½ starch, 3 medium-fat meat, 1½ fat

Pizza Burgers ⬤ VERY FAST ↑

    1 lb. lean ground venison, crumbled
    1 can (8 oz.) pizza sauce, divided
  ⅓ cup cut spicy pepperoni slices (1½ oz.),
         ¼-inch strips
    4 slices (1 oz. each) mozzarella cheese
    4 hamburger buns, split

4 servings

In medium mixing bowl, combine venison, ½ cup pizza sauce and the pepperoni. Shape mixture into four ½-inch-thick patties.

Heat 12-inch nonstick skillet over medium heat. Spray skillet with nonstick vegetable cooking spray. Add patties. Cook for 6 to 8 minutes, or until meat is desired doneness, turning patties over once. Top each patty with 1 slice cheese.

Place patties in buns and top evenly with remaining pizza sauce.

Per Serving: Calories: 521 • Protein: 34 g. • Carbohydrate: 26 g. • Fat: 30 g. • Cholesterol: 124 mg. • Sodium: 848 mg.
Exchanges: 1½ starch, 4 medium-fat meat, 1 vegetable, 2 fat

TO BROIL PATTIES, spray rack in broiler pan with nonstick vegetable cooking spray. Place patties on rack. Broil patties 4 to 5 inches from heat for 8 to 10 minutes, or until meat is desired doneness, turning patties over once.

Reuben Burgers ⬤ VERY FAST ↑

  ¼ cup Thousand Island salad dressing
    2 pita pocket loaves, cut in half crosswise
    1 lb. lean ground venison, crumbled
    1 teaspoon caraway seed
  ¼ teaspoon salt
  ¼ teaspoon pepper
    4 slices (1 oz. each) Swiss cheese
    1 can (8 oz.) sauerkraut, drained

4 servings

Spread dressing evenly inside pita pockets. Set aside.

In medium mixing bowl, combine venison, caraway seed, salt and pepper. Shape mixture into four ½-inch-thick patties.

Heat 12-inch nonstick skillet over medium heat. Spray skillet with nonstick vegetable cooking spray. Add patties. Cook for 6 to 8 minutes, or until meat is desired doneness, turning patties over once. Top each patty with 1 slice cheese. Place 1 patty in each pita pocket with sauerkraut.

Per Serving: Calories: 553 • Protein: 33 g. • Carbohydrate: 22 g. • Fat: 37 g. • Cholesterol: 127 mg. • Sodium: 654 mg.
Exchanges: 1½ starch, 4 medium-fat meat, 3 fat

TO GRILL PATTIES, place them on cooking grid over medium-direct heat. Grill for 8 to 10 minutes, or until meat is desired doneness, turning patties over once.

← Venison Sandwich Rolls 🔴 VERY FAST

2 sheets soft cracker bread
  (15-inch)
1 pkg. (8 oz.) spreadable onion
  and chive cream cheese
¾ lb. cooked venison top or
  bottom round roast, very
  thinly sliced
24 large spinach leaves, stems
  removed
1 jar (7 oz.) roasted red pepper,
  drained and cut into thin strips

4 servings

Cut each sheet of cracker bread in half to form 2 half circles. Spread cream cheese evenly over half circles. Arrange venison slices evenly over cream cheese to within 1 inch of edges. Top evenly with spinach leaves and pepper strips.

Beginning at short end of half circles, roll sandwiches up jelly-roll-style.

Per Serving: Calories: 583 • Protein: 41 g. • Carbohydrate: 57 g. • Fat: 21 g. • Cholesterol: 155 mg. • Sodium: 581 mg. Exchanges: 3½ starch, 4 very lean meat, 1 vegetable, 4 fat

Garlic Venison Sandwich with Cilantro Salsa

MARINADE:
  ½ cup dry red wine
  2 tablespoons packed brown sugar
  2 tablespoons lemon juice
  4 to 6 cloves garlic, minced
  ¼ teaspoon salt
  ⅛ teaspoon cayenne

  1-lb. venison top round steak, 1 inch thick

CILANTRO SALSA:
  4 to 6 cloves garlic
1¼ cups coarsely chopped fresh cilantro
  3 jalapeño peppers, seeded and coarsely chopped
  2 tablespoons olive oil
  1 tablespoon lemon juice
  1 teaspoon ground cumin
    Dash salt

  4 hamburger buns, split
    Tomato slices (optional)

4 servings

In large sealable plastic bag, combine marinade ingredients. Add steak, seal bag and turn to coat. Chill at least 1 hour, turning bag occasionally.

For salsa, process garlic in food processor or blender until finely chopped. Add remaining salsa ingredients. Process until nearly smooth. Transfer salsa to small bowl. Cover with plastic wrap. Set aside.

Prepare grill for medium direct heat. Drain and reserve marinade from steak. Grill steak, covered, for 15 to 18 minutes, or until meat is desired doneness, turning steak over once or twice and basting occasionally with marinade.

Thinly slice meat across grain. Fill buns evenly with steak slices. Top with salsa and tomato slices.

Per Serving: Calories: 358 • Protein: 30 g. • Carbohydrate: 29 g. • Fat: 12 g. • Cholesterol: 95 mg. • Sodium: 396 mg. Exchanges: 1½ starch, 3 very lean meat, 2¼ fat

Grilled Fajitas

½ cup fresh lime juice
¼ cup golden tequila or dark rum
3 tablespoons finely chopped onion
3 tablespoons vegetable oil
1 large clove garlic, minced
1½-lb. venison top round steak, 1 inch thick
2 large red peppers, seeded and cut into
    10 strips
1 large yellow pepper, seeded and cut into
    10 strips
1 large green pepper, seeded and cut into
    10 strips
6 flour tortillas (10-inch), warmed

GARNISHES (optional):
    Salsa
    Sour cream
    Guacamole
    Sliced green onions

6 servings

In large plastic food-storage bag, combine juice, tequila, onion, oil and garlic. Add steak, seal bag and turn to coat. Refrigerate overnight, turning bag occasionally.

Drain and discard marinade from steak. Prepare grill for medium direct heat. Grill steak, covered, for 15 to 18 minutes, or until meat is desired doneness, turning steak over once or twice. At same time, grill peppers for 6 to 8 minutes, or until tender and slightly blackened, turning peppers occasionally.

Thinly slice meat across grain. Spoon steak slices and peppers evenly in center of tortillas. Roll up and serve with desired garnishes.

Per Serving: Calories: 377 • Protein: 31 g. • Carbohydrate: 36 g. • Fat: 10 g. • Cholesterol: 96 mg. • Sodium: 311 mg.
Exchanges: 2 starch, 3 very lean meat, 1 vegetable, 2 fat

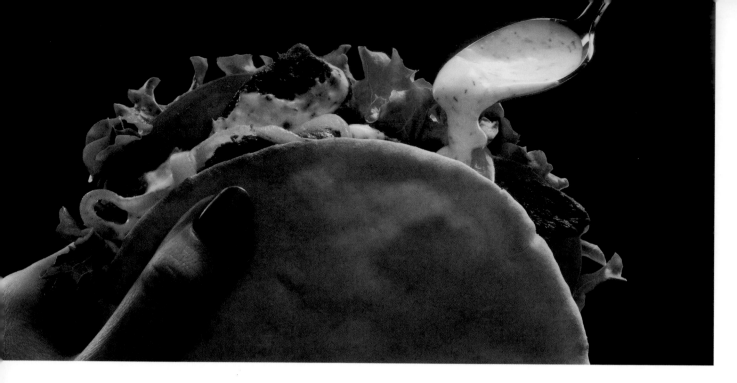

Barbecued Venison Sandwiches 🔵 LOW-FAT

This recipe makes enough for a crowd. If desired, you can freeze half of the meat after cooking it and halve the barbecue sauce ingredients for a smaller batch.

3-lb. venison top or bottom round
   roast
1 can (11½ oz.) tomato juice
1 large onion, sliced
½ teaspoon pepper

BARBECUE SAUCE:
1 small onion, chopped (½ cup)
½ cup water
3 cups catsup
⅔ cups packed brown sugar

½ cup Worcestershire sauce
½ cup white vinegar
2 tablespoons lemon juice
2 teaspoons celery seed
1 teaspoon salt
¼ to ½ teaspoon cayenne
½ teaspoon liquid smoke
   (optional)

24 hamburger buns

24 servings

Place roast in 6-quart Dutch oven. Add tomato juice, onion and pepper. Bring to a boil over high heat. Reduce heat to low. Cover. Simmer for 1 to 1½ hours, or until meat is tender, turning meat occasionally.

Remove roast from pan and let stand until meat is cool enough to handle. (If desired, refrigerate roast overnight.) Using fork, shred meat along grain. Set aside.

To make sauce, combine onion and water in 4-quart saucepan. Cook over medium heat for 4 to 6 minutes, or until onion is tender and water is boiled off, stirring frequently. Stir in remaining sauce ingredients. Bring to a boil. Reduce heat to low. Simmer for 10 to 15 minutes, or until flavors are blended.

In 6-quart Dutch oven, combine shredded venison and barbecue sauce. Cook over medium heat for 10 to 15 minutes, or until heated through, stirring occasionally. Spoon mixture into hamburger buns to serve.

TIP: Sauce can be made ahead and refrigerated until ready to use.

Per Serving: Calories: 261 • Protein: 18 g. • Carbohydrate: 39 g. • Fat: 4 g.
• Cholesterol: 48 mg. • Sodium: 828 mg.
Exchanges: 1½ starch, 1½ very lean meat, 2 vegetable, ½ fat

Venison Gyros 🔵 VERY FAST ↑

DRESSING:
1 cup plain low-fat yogurt
½ teaspoon dried dill weed
½ teaspoon garlic powder

2 tablespoons garlic-flavored oil
   or olive oil
1-lb. venison top round steak
   (1 inch thick), cut into
   2 × ¼-inch slices
1 small onion, sliced and
   separated into rings
2 cloves garlic, minced
1 teaspoon dried oregano leaves
4 pita pocket loaves, split open
4 lettuce leaves
8 slices tomato

4 servings

In 2-cup measure, combine dressing ingredients. Set aside. In 12-inch nonstick skillet, heat oil over medium-high heat. Add venison, onion, garlic and oregano. Cook for 4 to 6 minutes, or until meat is no longer pink and onion is tender, stirring frequently. Remove from heat.

Line pitas with lettuce leaves and tomato slices. Spoon meat mixture evenly into pitas. Top with dressing.

Per Serving: Calories: 413 • Protein: 35 g.
• Carbohydrate: 41 g. • Fat: 11 g.
• Cholesterol: 99 mg. • Sodium: 411 mg.
Exchanges: 2 starch, 3 very lean meat,
1½ vegetable, ⅓ low-fat milk, 2 fat

French Dip

3- lb. venison top or bottom round
    roast
4 cloves garlic, cut into slivers
4 cups beef or venison stock
4 teaspoons beef bouillon
    granules
1/2 teaspoon pepper
10 to 12 hoagie buns, split

10 to 12 servings

Pierce roast several times with tip of sharp knife. Insert garlic slivers into holes made by knife. Place roast in 6-quart Dutch oven. Add stock, bouillon and pepper.

Bring to a boil over high heat. Reduce heat to low. Cover. Simmer for 1 to 1½ hours, or until meat is tender, turning meat occasionally. Remove roast from pan. Let stand for 10 minutes. Cut meat into very thin slices.

Strain liquid in pan through fine-mesh sieve. Return liquid to pan. Add sliced meat to liquid. (Recipe can be prepared to this point, then refrigerated and reheated when ready to use.) Heat meat mixture over medium-low heat for 10 to 12 minutes, or until hot. Using slotted spoon, spoon meat evenly into hoagie buns. Serve with small dish of cooking liquid for dipping.

TIP: If additional dipping liquid is desired, add 1 cup of water and 1½ teaspoons beef bouillon granules.

Per Serving: Calories: 315 • Protein: 32 g. • Carbohydrate: 32 g. • Fat: 5 g.
• Cholesterol: 96 mg. • Sodium: 660 mg.
Exchanges: 2¼ starch, 3 very lean meat, 1 fat

Salads

Antipasto Salad →

8 oz. fresh mushrooms, quartered
2 cups broccoli flowerets, blanched*
2 medium carrots, cut into 2 × ¼-inch strips (1 cup)
1 cup thin cucumber slices
1 bottle (8 oz.) Italian dressing
1 head green leaf lettuce, torn into bite-size pieces
¾ lb. venison summer sausage, cut into ½-inch cubes
8 oz. Cheddar cheese, cut into ½-inch cubes
1 can (14 oz.) whole artichoke hearts in water, drained and halved
1 can (14 oz.) whole baby corn, drained and halved
1 can (6 oz.) pitted ripe olives, drained

6 servings

Place mushrooms, broccoli, carrots and cucumber in separate small bowls. Pour ¼ cup dressing over each vegetable, stirring to coat. Cover bowls with plastic wrap. Chill.

Arrange lettuce on large serving platter. Arrange marinated vegetables, sausage, cheese, artichoke hearts, corn and olives as desired on lettuce. Drizzle salad with any remaining dressing.

See Venison Rotini Salad, page 98, for blanching technique.

Nutritional information not available due to summer sausage.

← Warm Venison-Black Bean Salad 🍅 VERY FAST

1 lb. lean ground venison, crumbled
½ cup coarsely chopped red onion
2 jalapeño peppers, sliced and seeded
2 cloves garlic, minced
2 cans (15 oz. each) black beans, rinsed and drained
2 medium tomatoes, seeded and chopped
2 tablespoons fresh lime juice
1 teaspoon ground cumin
½ teaspoon dried oregano leaves
½ teaspoon salt
¼ teaspoon pepper
⅛ to ¼ teaspoon cayenne
⅓ cup snipped fresh cilantro
6 corn tortillas (6-inch)
1 avocado, peeled and sliced

6 servings

In 12-inch nonstick skillet, cook venison, onion, jalapeños and garlic over medium heat for 6 to 8 minutes, or until meat is no longer pink, stirring occasionally. Drain. Stir in beans, tomatoes, juice, cumin, oregano, salt, pepper and cayenne. Cook for 2 to 3 minutes, or until heated through, stirring occasionally. Stir in cilantro.

Warm tortillas as directed on package. Spoon salad over tortillas in individual servings. Garnish salads with avocado slices.

Per Serving: Calories: 365 • Protein: 22 g. • Carbohydrate: 32 g. • Fat: 17 g. • Cholesterol: 63 mg. • Sodium: 493 mg.
Exchanges: 1¾ starch, 2 medium-fat meat, 1 vegetable, 1½ fat

Caesar Salad with Venison

DRESSING:

¼ cup red wine vinegar

3 tablespoons garlic-flavored oil

¼ to ½ teaspoon seasoned salt

¼ teaspoon Worcestershire sauce

¼ teaspoon dry mustard

1 tablespoon garlic-flavored oil

1-lb. venison top or bottom round roast, cut into ¾-inch cubes

1 head romaine, coarsely torn (8 cups)

1 cup prepared croutons

⅓ cup shredded fresh Parmesan cheese

6 anchovy fillets, coarsely chopped

2 hard-cooked eggs, sliced

6 to 8 servings

In 1-cup measure, whisk together dressing ingredients. Set aside.

In 12-inch nonstick skillet, heat 1 tablespoon oil over medium-high heat. Add venison. Cook for 4 to 6 minutes, or until meat is no longer pink, stirring occasionally. Drain. Cool slightly. In medium mixing bowl, combine venison cubes and dressing. Toss to coat. Cover with plastic wrap. Chill, stirring occasionally.

In large mixing bowl or salad bowl, combine romaine, croutons, Parmesan cheese, anchovies and venison mixture. Toss to combine. Top with sliced eggs.

Per Serving: Calories: 197 • Protein: 18 g. • Carbohydrate: 5 g. • Fat: 11 g. • Cholesterol: 106 mg. • Sodium: 315 mg.
Exchanges: ¼ starch, 2¼ very lean meat, ½ vegetable, 2¼ fat

Grilled Greek Salad →

1-lb. venison top or bottom round
    steak, 1 inch thick
1 cup Italian dressing, divided
3 cups cubed Italian bread
    (1-inch cubes)
3 tablespoons butter or
    margarine, melted
¼ teaspoon garlic powder
3 cups torn fresh spinach
2 cups torn romaine
2 medium tomatoes, seeded and
    chopped (2 cups)
1 can (15 oz.) garbanzo beans,
    rinsed and drained
1 medium green, red or yellow
    pepper, seeded and sliced
1 cup crumbled feta cheese
½ cup sliced green onions
⅓ cup sliced Greek or black olives

8 servings

Place venison in shallow dish. Pour ½ cup dressing over venison, turning to coat. Cover with plastic wrap. Chill at least 30 minutes, turning occasionally.

Heat oven to 350°F. Place bread cubes in medium mixing bowl. In 1-cup measure, combine butter and garlic powder. Drizzle over bread cubes. Toss cubes to coat completely. Spread cubes in single layer on baking sheet. Bake for 15 to 18 minutes, or until cubes are lightly browned, stirring occasionally. Set croutons aside.

Prepare grill for medium direct heat. Spray cooking grid with nonstick vegetable cooking spray. Grill steak for 15 to 18 minutes, or until meat is desired doneness, turning steak over once or twice. Let stand for 5 minutes before slicing. Slice meat across grain into 2 × 1 × ¼-inch strips.

In large mixing bowl or salad bowl, combine venison strips, croutons and remaining ingredients. Add remaining ½ cup dressing. Toss to coat.

Per Serving: Calories: 363 • Protein: 20 g.
• Carbohydrate: 19 g. • Fat: 24 g.
• Cholesterol: 74 mg. • Sodium: 781 mg.
Exchanges: 1 starch, 2¼ very lean meat,
¾ vegetable, 4½ fat

Ramen Noodle-Cabbage Salad

1-lb. venison top or bottom round
    steak, 1 inch thick
1 tablespoon rice vinegar
½ teaspoon five-spice powder
¼ teaspoon salt
1 pkg. (3 oz.) chicken-flavored
    Ramen noodle soup mix,
    uncooked

DRESSING:
⅓ cup olive oil

¼ cup rice vinegar or white vinegar
2 tablespoons sugar
    Seasoning packet from soup mix
1 teaspoon salt
¼ teaspoon pepper

6 cups chopped white cabbage
½ medium red onion, sliced
½ cup sliced almonds, toasted*

6 servings

Sprinkle both sides of steak with vinegar. Sprinkle both sides evenly with five-spice powder and salt. Place steak on rack in broiler pan. Broil steak 4 to 5 inches from heat for 15 to 18 minutes, or until desired doneness, turning steak over once. Slice steak across grain into 3 × 1 × ¼-inch strips. Place strips in large mixing bowl or salad bowl. Set aside.

In 2-cup measure, whisk together dressing ingredients. Add to venison. Toss to coat. Add cabbage and onion. Toss to combine. Cover with plastic wrap. Refrigerate salad 2 to 3 hours, tossing occasionally. Just before serving, crumble uncooked Ramen noodles over salad and add almonds. Toss to combine.

To toast almonds, spread them on baking sheet and bake at 350 °F for 5 to 7 minutes, stirring occasionally.

Per Serving: Calories: 349 • Protein: 21 g. • Carbohydrate: 21 g. • Fat: 21 g.
• Cholesterol: 64 mg. • Sodium: 813 mg.
Exchanges: ¾ starch, 2¼ very lean meat, 1 vegetable, 4 fat

Venison Rotini Salad ⏱FAST ↑

1 pkg. (16 oz.) uncooked rotini pasta
3/4 lb. venison summer sausage, cut into 1/2-inch
    cubes
2 medium tomatoes, seeded and chopped (2 cups)
2 cups broccoli flowerets, fresh or blanched*
1 1/2 cups shredded Cheddar cheese
1/2 cup sliced green onions
1 cup Italian dressing or sun-dried tomato dressing

8 to 10 servings

Prepare pasta as directed on package. Rinse with
cold water. Drain. Place rotini in large mixing bowl
or salad bowl. Add sausage, tomatoes, broccoli,
cheese and onions. Toss to combine. Pour dressing
over salad. Toss to coat. Serve immediately or chill
1 or 2 hours.

*To blanch broccoli, bring several cups of water to
a boil in large saucepan. Plunge broccoli in boiling
water for 2 to 3 minutes, or until color brightens.
Remove broccoli from water with slotted spoon.
Immediately plunge broccoli into ice water. Drain.*

TIP: The pasta will absorb the dressing if the salad
is made too far in advance. If you want to make the
salad ahead of time, combine all salad ingredients,
except cheese and dressing. Add cheese and dressing
just before serving.

Nutritional information not available due to summer sausage.

Broccoli-Venison Salad ↑

*This easy salad is perfect to take to a picnic or potluck. It can be
made up to a day ahead, too.*

2 cups water
6 cups coarsely chopped broccoli (1 lb.)
1 1/2 cups cubed cooked venison roast (1/2-inch cubes)
1 1/2 cups chopped celery
1/2 cup sliced green onions
1/2 cup sliced pimiento-stuffed green olives
3 hard-cooked eggs, chopped

DRESSING:
1 1/2 cups mayonnaise
1/3 cup 2% milk
1 teaspoon dried dill weed
1 teaspoon lemon juice
1/8 teaspoon salt

8 servings

In 3-quart saucepan, bring water to a boil over high
heat. Stir in broccoli. Reduce heat to medium. Simmer for 10 to 12 minutes, or until broccoli is tender-
crisp. Drain. Rinse broccoli with cold water. Drain.

In large mixing bowl or salad bowl, combine broccoli,
venison, celery, onions, olives and eggs. In small mixing bowl, whisk together dressing ingredients. Pour
dressing over salad. Toss to coat. Cover with plastic
wrap. Chill at least 1 hour.

Per Serving: Calories: 404 • Protein: 13 g. • Carbohydrate: 6 g.
• Fat: 37 g. • Cholesterol: 135 mg. • Sodium: 552 mg.
Exchanges: 1 1/2 very lean meat, 1 vegetable, 7 1/4 fat

Raspberry Venison Salad FAST

DRESSING:
- 1 pkg. (10 oz.) frozen raspberries in syrup, defrosted
- 1/3 cup raspberry vinegar
- 2 tablespoons Dijon mustard
- 2 tablespoons nonfat plain yogurt
- 1 tablespoon finely chopped onion
- 1 small clove garlic, minced
- 1 cup vegetable oil

SALAD:
- 1 lb. venison top round, cut into 2 × 1 × 1/8-inch strips
- 4 cups mixed baby greens
- 1/2 medium red onion, thinly sliced
- 4 oz. chèvre cheese*, cut into 1/2-inch cubes
- Fresh raspberries

4 servings

In food processor or blender, combine all dressing ingredients, except oil. Process until smooth. With machine running, slowly add oil in thin stream. Process until well blended. Set aside.

Heat 12-inch nonstick skillet over medium-high heat. Spray skillet with nonstick vegetable cooking spray. Add venison strips. Cook for 4 to 6 minutes, or until meat is no longer pink, stirring frequently. Drain.

Arrange greens on large serving platter. Add venison, onion and cheese. Toss to combine. Garnish with fresh raspberries. Serve with dressing. (Store any remaining dressing in refrigerator in covered container.)

Chèvre is a white cheese made from goat's milk. (Chèvre means "goat" in French.) It has a tart flavor, and ranges in texture from moist and creamy to dry and semifirm.

Per Serving with 3 tablespoons dressing: Calories: 426 • Protein: 33 g. • Carbohydrate: 11 g. • Fat: 28 g. • Cholesterol: 118 mg. • Sodium: 255 mg.
Exchanges: 4 very lean meat, 1 vegetable, 1/4 fruit, 5 1/2 fat

← Sesame Venison Salad

Sesame Venison Salad

1 lb. venison tenderloin, cut
   crosswise into ¼-inch slices

DRESSING:

2 tablespoons vegetable oil
2 tablespoons sesame oil
2 tablespoons soy sauce
2 tablespoons rice vinegar
1 tablespoon sesame seed
1 tablespoon grated fresh
   gingerroot
2 teaspoons packed brown sugar
1 teaspoon grated fresh lemon
   peel
1 teaspoon hot chili oil
1 clove garlic, minced

1 carrot, cut into 2 × ¼-inch
   strips (¾ cup)
½ medium red pepper, seeded and
   cut into thin strips
½ medium red onion, cut into thin
   wedges and separated
½ cup walnut halves, toasted*
4 cups mixed baby greens

4 servings

Heat 12-inch skillet over medium-high heat. Spray skillet with non-stick vegetable cooking spray. Add venison slices. Cook for 4 to 6 minutes, or until meat is no longer pink, stirring frequently. Drain. Set aside.

In medium mixing bowl, combine dressing ingredients. Whisk to blend. Stir in venison. Let stand for 15 minutes, stirring occasionally. Stir in carrot, red pepper, onion and walnuts. Toss to coat. Arrange greens evenly on individual serving plates. Spoon salad evenly over greens.

To toast walnut halves, spread them on baking sheet and bake at 375°F for 7 to 10 minutes, stirring occasionally.

Per Serving: Calories: 407 • Protein: 30 g.
• Carbohydrate: 13 g. • Fat: 27 g.
• Cholesterol: 95 mg. • Sodium: 578 mg.
Exchanges: 3½ very lean meat,
1¼ vegetable, 5¼ fat

Wild Rice Salad

SALAD:

2 cups cooked wild rice
1½ cups shredded or cubed
   cooked venison
½ cup chopped tart green apple
½ cup dried cherries or
   cranberries
½ cup walnut pieces
½ cup chopped carrot
½ cup chopped red onion
1 teaspoon snipped fresh
   tarragon leaves

DRESSING:

3 tablespoons olive oil
2 tablespoons tarragon vinegar
2 tablespoons fresh lemon juice
1 teaspoon Dijon mustard
½ teaspoon Worcestershire
   sauce
¼ teaspoon salt
¼ teaspoon pepper

4 to 6 servings

In large mixing bowl or salad bowl, combine all salad ingredients. Set aside. In small mixing bowl, combine all dressing ingredients. Whisk well. Add dressing to salad and toss to coat. Cover with plastic wrap. Chill. Serve salad on lettuce-lined plates.

Per Serving: Calories: 282 • Protein: 15 g. • Carbohydrate: 26 g. • Fat: 14 g.
• Cholesterol: 40 mg. • Sodium: 142 mg.
Exchanges: 1 starch, 1½ very lean meat, ½ vegetable, ½ fruit, 3 fat

Oriental Salad with Fried Wontons

2 tablespoons garlic-flavored oil
1 lb. venison top or bottom round, cut into 2 × ½ × ¼-inch strips
⅓ cup vegetable oil
⅓ cup white wine vinegar
¼ cup soy sauce
3 tablespoons sugar
1 tablespoon grated fresh gingerroot
1 tablespoon sesame seed
4 cups shredded white cabbage
1 cup halved snow pea pods
½ cup shredded carrot
4 oz. wonton skins, cut into 3½ × ¾-inch strips
½ cup slivered almonds, toasted*

6 servings

In 12-inch skillet, heat garlic-flavored oil over medium heat. Add venison. Cook for 4 to 6 minutes, or until venison is no longer pink, stirring occasionally. Drain. Set aside.

In 2-cup measure, combine vegetable oil, vinegar, soy sauce, sugar, gingerroot and sesame seed. Whisk well. Set dressing aside.

Mound cabbage, pea pods and carrot in center of serving platter. Top with venison strips. Cover with plastic wrap. Chill. Meanwhile, heat 2 inches oil in wok or medium, heavy saucepan to 375°F. Drop one-third of wonton strips into hot oil. Cook for 20 to 30 seconds, or until wontons are browned and crisp. Using slotted spoon, immediately remove wontons to paper-towel-lined plate. Repeat with remaining wontons.

Arrange fried wontons around outer edge of salad. Sprinkle almonds over top. Serve salad with dressing.

To toast almonds, spread them on baking sheet and bake at 350°F for 6 to 8 minutes, stirring occasionally.

Per Serving: Calories: 414 • Protein: 23 g. • Carbohydrate: 27 g. • Fat: 24 g. • Cholesterol: 65 mg. • Sodium: 839 mg.
Exchanges: ¾ starch, 2½ very lean meat, 1½ vegetable, 4¾ fat

Venison Sausages & Smokehouse Specialties

There are few things more satisfying than making your own sausages, whether fresh or smoked, and doing the job well.

The arts of sausage making and smoking are not as difficult as you may think. Good mail-order sources make special sausage-making equipment and ingredients available to anyone. All it takes is a little patience and practice to produce wholesome, delicious sausages and jerky.

You can use a standard covered grill to smoke, convert an old refrigerator into a smoker or buy a deluxe insulated smokehouse. Recipes on the following pages were developed using an insulated smoker. Just keep in mind that whatever you use, your smoking can be affected by wind and weather.

Temperature control when smoking is extremely important for proper drying of sausages and for quality control. Most fresh sausages are cooked by methods other than smoking. They may be smoked at low temperatures for flavoring, but are later grilled, broiled or panfried. Salami and other cured sausages, however, receive no further cooking.

Because low smokehouse temperatures and airtight casings create an ideal environment for bacteria growth, we recommend adding *cure* (page 105) to all sausage that is smoked. This prevents the growth of organisms that cause food poisoning. Cure can be found in stores that specialize in smoking and outdoor cooking equipment (see page 128).

On the following pages, we explain how to make several fresh venison sausages and include detailed step-by-step sequences for using natural and synthetic casings. We'll take you through the steps necessary to make your own cured, smoked salami and jerky. Start with the basics, and you'll have great success making your own smoked specialties.

SAUSAGE-MAKING SUPPLIES & EQUIPMENT include (1) optional heavy-duty sausage stuffer and stuffing horns, helpful for large quantities; (2) large nonmetallic mixing bowl or tub; (3) kitchen scale; (4) kitchen twine; (5) sausage casings; (6) meat grinder with 2 grinding plates; and specialty ingredients and optional equipment for cured sausages, including (7) powdered dextrose, (8) soy protein concentrate, (9) premixed cure/seasoning blends, (10) curing powder or curing salt, and (11) sausage pricker for eliminating air bubbles in stuffed sausage.

Venison Sausages

For venison sausages, use trimmed meat from any part of the animal; the meat doesn't need to be tender. Generally, fatty pork butt or plain pork fat is added to the lean meat for moisture and flavor. Avoid using deer fat because it can give a gamey flavor to sausages. Be sure to specify hard pork *back fat* when you order the fat from your butcher; tell the butcher what you'll be using it for to be sure you get the right thing. (Back fat is not the same as *fatback,* which is fat that has been salted and dried.) Lard is too soft and will produce a greasy sausage. It should not be used.

Keep meat-grinder blades sharp when grinding meat for sausage. Dull blades squeeze juices from the meat, resulting in dry, less-flavorful sausage.

If your grinder slows down during use or if the texture of the meat suddenly becomes fine and mushy, partially disassemble the grinder and check the blades and plate. Sinew and other tough material can get caught in the mechanism, causing poor performance. Clean the blade and plate, then continue.

You may need some help when making sausages. One person can press the meat through the sausage stuffer, while the other guides the casings off the horn and twists the links.

1. GRIND lean meat separately from fat for juicier fresh sausages. Cut fat into chunks, partially freeze it, then grind it finer than the meat. Mix ground meat and ground fat together. This way, the fat will be more evenly distributed and there won't be any large pieces in your sausage.

2. USE a cure for all sausages that will be smoked, to prevent botulism, a type of food poisoning. For a fresh-sausage recipe that makes 5 pounds, *substitute* 8 level teaspoons Morton® TenderQuick® mix for 5½ level teaspoons canning/pickling salt; or, *add* 1 level teaspoon Insta Cure No. 1 (formerly Prague Powder No. 1) to the salt already in recipe.

3. CHOOSE (1) lamb casings for breakfast sausages; (2) collagen casings for snack sticks; (3) hog casings for Polish-size sausages; or (4) synthetic-fibrous casings for salami. Fresh-sausage recipes need not be cased; form into (5) patties, and fry, grill or broil.

Using Synthetic & Natural Casings

Synthetic casings used in this book include 22 mm and 32 mm collagen casings, which are edible, and 3½-inch synthetic-fibrous casings, which are peeled and discarded before the sausage is eaten. Salami-size casings can also be made from clean muslin. Before stuffing, sew one end shut in a half circle and turn right side out to prevent unraveling. Stuff tightly and tie off as directed below.

Natural sausage casings include lamb casings (22 to 24 mm), which are used for breakfast links, and hog casings (32 to 35 mm is a common size), which are used for Italian, Polish and country-style links. A butcher shop that specializes in sausages may sell you a hank, a bundle of casings packed in salt. You can also order casings from specialty sources (see page 128).

The casing you select is based on the sausage you'll be making. Natural casings are usually used for fresh sausages, since they are tender and edible. Synthetic-fibrous casings are perfect for salami, and are easier to find than natural alternatives. Collagen casings are available for both fresh and smoked sausages in sizes for small links or bratwurst. They are easier to use than natural casings, but they don't hold a twist well and may need to be hand tied at the ends.

1. SOAK synthetic-fibrous casings in a mixture of 3 table-spoons white vinegar to 2 quarts lukewarm water for 30 minutes, or as directed by manufacturer. The vinegar helps the casing to peel smoothly from the finished salami and helps prevent mold growth. Wet a homemade muslin casing before stuffing.

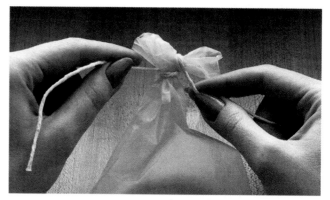

2. WRAP the middle of a 20-inch piece of kitchen string tightly around one end of the casing several times; then fan out the end like butterfly wings. Wrap one end of the string tightly around one wing several times. Repeat on the other side. Wrap both ends of string around main neck again. Tie securely.

3. STUFF with sausage mixture by hand or with a stuffing horn. Pack casing tightly, squeezing to force out air pockets. Tie off with butterfly knot; make loop in string for hanging sausage. If there are small air bubbles trapped under the surface, pierce casing with sterilized needle or sausage pricker.

1. SPREAD OUT a hank of salted casings carefully on clean work surface. Find the beginning of the hank, and gently pull one length out of the bundle until it is free, being careful not to twist the remainder of the lengths. Remove as many lengths as you need. Resalt and freeze the remainder for future use.

2. OPEN one end of the casing, and slip the end over a faucet. Hold your hand over the casing to keep it from slipping off. Run a steady, medium stream of cold water through the casing until it is completely filled and the water runs through. Continue flushing for a few minutes. Rinse the outside of the casing.

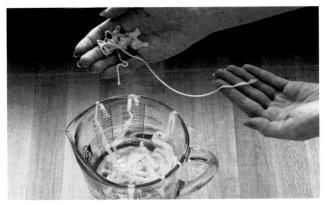

3. PLACE the rinsed casing in a large measuring cup filled with cold water after draining out all water and air from the casing. Let one end of the casing hang over the edge of the cup. Rinse remaining casings, adding them to the measuring cup, until you've rinsed all the casings you will need.

4. SLIP one end of a rinsed, wet casing over the sausage-stuffing horn; push until the end of the casing is at the back end of the horn. Continue pushing until the entire length is gathered onto the horn. Pull the casing forward until about 1 inch hangs over the open end of the horn.

5. TURN the crank of the sausage stuffer slowly until some of the sausage mixture comes out of the horn. Tie off the end of the casing with kitchen string, pinching off a small bit of meat. The pinching helps eliminate air at the end of the link. Continue cranking until sausage is desired length; have a helper guide the link away from the horn.

6. TWIST the first link several times; then crank until a second link is formed. Support both links with one hand while using the other to keep the casing on the horn until it is firmly filled. Be sure to let the casing slip off easily before it overfills and breaks. Continue twisting and filling; keep casings on horn wet so they slip off without sticking.

Fresh Sausages

Fresh sausages are probably the easiest to make, since they require few special ingredients and no smoking. Fresh sausage mixtures can be stuffed into casings or formed into patties or logs. They should be kept in the refrigerator and used within 2 or 3 days, or frozen for future use.

Spicy Bratwurst-style Sausage

3 lbs. lean ground venison, crumbled
3 lbs. ground pork, crumbled
2 tablespoons canning/pickling salt
2 tablespoons dried parsley flakes
1 tablespoon crushed red pepper flakes
1 tablespoon dried onion flakes
2 teaspoons garlic powder
1 teaspoon freshly ground pepper
Collagen casings (32 mm) for fresh sausage, or natural hog casings (29 to 32 mm)

24 sausages
(about 4 oz. each)

In large mixing bowl, combine ground venison and ground pork. In small mixing bowl, combine remaining ingredients, except casings. Sprinkle seasoning mixture evenly over meat. Mix by hand until ingredients are evenly distributed. Cover with plastic wrap. Refrigerate until ready to stuff.

Prepare and stuff casings as directed for natural casings (page 107), using a ¾-inch horn and twisting off in 6-inch links. (It may be necessary to hand tie ends of each link with kitchen string if collagen casings are used.) If any air pockets remain on surface of sausages, pierce the casing with a sterilized sausage pricker or needle.

To prepare, place desired number of sausages in saucepan with 1 inch of water or beer. Bring to a boil over high heat. Reduce heat to medium. Cover. Simmer for 4 to 6 minutes, or until sausages are firm. Sausages may be grilled, or cooled, sliced and used in recipes as desired.

Per Sausage: Calories: 299 • Protein: 20 g. • Carbohydrate: <1 g. • Fat: 23 g.
• Cholesterol: 92 mg. • Sodium: 424 mg.
Exchanges: 3 medium-fat meat, 1½ fat

← Fresh Breakfast Links

2 lbs. lean ground venison, crumbled
2 lbs. ground pork, crumbled
⅓ cup plus 2 tablespoons ice water
1½ tablespoons salt
1 teaspoon white pepper
1 teaspoon rubbed sage
1 teaspoon ground thyme
¼ teaspoon ground nutmeg
¼ teaspoon ground ginger
Collagen casings (22 mm) for fresh sausage, or natural sheep casings (22 to 24 mm)

44 sausages
(about 1½ oz. each)

In large mixing bowl, combine ground venison and ground pork. In small mixing bowl, combine remaining ingredients, except casings. Add to meat mixture. Mix by hand until ingredients are evenly distributed. Cover with plastic wrap. Refrigerate until ready to stuff.

Prepare and stuff casings as directed for natural casings (page 107), using a ½-inch horn and twisting off in 4-inch links. (It may be necessary to hand tie ends of each link with kitchen string if collagen casings are used.) If any air pockets remain on surface of sausages, pierce the casing with a sterilized sausage pricker or needle. Sausages may be panfried or grilled. Wrap tightly and freeze any remaining sausages for future use.

Variation: For sausage patties, prepare recipe as directed above, except omit casings. Shape meat mixture evenly into patties. Freeze patties in sealable plastic bags between layers of wax paper.

Per Sausage: Calories: 108 • Protein: 7 g. • Carbohydrate: 0 g. • Fat: 8 g.
• Cholesterol: 33 mg. • Sodium: 245 mg.
Exchanges: 1 medium-fat meat, ¾ fat

Lean Fresh Ground Sausage

This easy sausage recipe can be formed into patties or used in any recipe that calls for fresh ground sausage.

1 lb. lean ground venison, crumbled
1 teaspoon fennel seed
1 teaspoon salt
½ teaspoon garlic powder
¼ to ½ teaspoon crushed red pepper flakes

4 servings

In medium mixing bowl, combine all ingredients. Mix well. Shape mixture into eight 3-inch patties. In 12-inch nonstick skillet, cook patties over medium heat for 5 to 6 minutes, or until meat is no longer pink in center, turning patties over once or twice.

TIP: Patties can be frozen in sealable plastic bags between layers of wax paper. To prepare from frozen state, cook patties in nonstick skillet over medium-low heat for 18 to 20 minutes, or until meat is no longer pink in center, turning patties over once or twice.

Per Serving: Calories: 299 • Protein: 22 g.
• Carbohydrate: 1 g. • Fat: 23 g.
• Cholesterol: 101 mg. • Sodium: 598 mg.
Exchanges: 3 medium-fat meat, 1½ fat

Smoking Techniques

Cold smoking is done at temperatures below 120°F, and works well for drying and flavoring fresh sausages prior to cooking. Hot smoking, or *smoke cooking,* is generally done at temperatures from 150° to 250°F, and is used to fully cook meats while imparting a smoky flavor.

Many types of smokers are available, ranging from sheet-aluminum smokers with an electric hot plate to produce smoke and limited heat, to charcoal or electric-powered water smokers. You can also use a covered grill as a hot smoker. *America's Favorite Fish Recipes, Cleaning & Cooking Fish,* and *Dressing & Cooking Wild Game,* all published by The Hunting & Fishing Library®, go into more detail about these alternative types of smokers.

All smokers require wood to produce smoke. Sports stores and specialty catalogs (see page 128) sell chips and sawdust of various hardwoods, including hickory, cherry, alder, apple and mesquite. You can also use corncobs or hardwood trimmings. Professionals prefer sawdust to larger pieces, because it provides a more even *smudge,* or smoke density. For maximum smoke production, wood chips and trimmings should be soaked in water before use; sawdust should be slightly dampened.

Temperature control is especially important when cooking summer sausage in a smoker, because the

sausage receives no further cooking. An insulated electric smokehouse is perfect for this, because the temperature is easy to adjust and maintain. Monitor the smoker temperature constantly with an instant-read or oven thermometer. A digital thermometer is useful for monitoring the internal temperature of sausage during smoking.

USE (1) wood chips, tree trimmings or smoking sawdust, to provide smoke. Use (2) digital thermometer to monitor internal temperature of summer sausage or large cuts of meat without opening the smoker, which causes heat loss; and (3) instant-read thermometer to monitor smoker temperature. Insert thermometer into vent hole on smoker or hole designed for thermometer.

SMOKING EQUIPMENT AND SUPPLIES include (1) insulated electric smokehouse, with variable-power heat source; (2) electric sheet-aluminum smoker;

(3) charcoal or electric water smoker, with water pan above heat source to keep smoker air moist.

Smoked Cajun Sausage

3 lbs. lean ground venison, crumbled
3 lbs. ground pork, crumbled
⅔ cup soy protein concentrate
2 tablespoons Morton® TenderQuick® mix
1 tablespoon paprika
1 tablespoon minced dehydrated onions
1 tablespoon cayenne
1 tablespoon salt
2 teaspoons black pepper
2 teaspoons white pepper
2 teaspoons garlic powder
1 teaspoon ground cumin
1 teaspoon thyme leaves
1½ to 3 cups hickory wood chips
Collagen casings (32 mm) for smoked sausages, or natural hog casings (29 to 32 mm)

24 sausages

Nutritional information not available because there is no nutritional data available for soy protein concentrate or TenderQuick mix.

In large nonmetallic mixing bowl, combine ground venison and ground pork. In small mixing bowl, combine remaining ingredients, except wood chips and casings. Add to meat mixture. Mix by hand until ingredients are evenly distributed. Cover with plastic wrap. Refrigerate until ready to stuff.

Place wood chips in large mixing bowl. Cover with water. Soak chips for 1 hour. Place oven thermometer in smoker. Heat smoker until temperature registers 130°F. Prepare and stuff casings as directed for natural casings (page 107), using a ¾-inch horn and twisting off in 6-inch links. (It may be necessary to hand tie ends of each link with kitchen string if collagen casings are used.) If any air pockets remain on surface of sausages, pierce the casing with a sterilized sausage pricker or needle.

Drain wood chips. Hang sausages on smokehouse sticks, spacing at least 1 inch apart. Place in smoker. Open damper. Maintain temperature at 130°F for 30 minutes, or until surface of sausages is dry. Partially close damper to raise temperature to 165°F. Place wood chips in smoker. Smoke at 165°F for 2½ to 4 hours, or until internal temperature of largest sausage registers 152°F. (Times are approximate and will vary, depending upon size and diameter of sausages, weather conditions and type of smoker used.)

Remove sausages from smoker and flush sausages with cold water until internal temperature registers 120°F. Store sausages, tightly wrapped, in refrigerator for no longer than 1 week, or wrap tightly and freeze up to 2 months for best quality.

NOTE: See page 128 for mail-order source for soy protein concentrate.

111

8 lbs. lean ground venison, crumbled
2 lbs. pork back fat, cut into 1-inch pieces
6 oz. Fermento
6 tablespoons canning/pickling salt
¼ cup powdered dextrose
1 tablespoon freshly ground pepper
1 tablespoon ground coriander
2 level teaspoons Insta Cure No. 1 (formerly Prague Powder No. 1)
1 teaspoon ground ginger
1 teaspoon dry mustard
1 teaspoon garlic powder
1½ to 3 cups hickory wood chips
6 to 8 synthetic-fibrous casings, 3½ × 12 inches

About 10 lbs. (2 oz. per serving)

Nutritional information not available because there is no nutritional data available for Fermento or Insta Cure No. 1.

In large nonmetallic mixing bowl, combine ground meat and back fat. In medium mixing bowl, combine remaining ingredients, except wood chips and casings. Add to meat mixture. Mix by hand until ingredients are evenly distributed. Cover with plastic wrap. Refrigerate 24 hours.

Place wood chips in large mixing bowl. Cover with water. Soak chips for 1 hour. Soak casings as directed for synthetic casings (page 106). Grind meat mixture through a 3/16-inch plate. Re-cover meat. Refrigerate until ready to stuff.

Place oven thermometer in smoker. Heat smoker until temperature registers 130°F. While smoker heats, prepare and stuff casings as directed for synthetic casings (page 106), to within 2 inches of top. Secure with butterfly knot as directed for synthetic casings (page 106). If any air pockets remain on surface of sausages, pierce the casing with a sterilized sausage pricker or needle.

Drain wood chips. Hang sausages on smokehouse sticks, spacing at least 1 inch apart. Place in smoker. Open damper. Maintain temperature at 130°F for 30 minutes, or until surface of sausages is dry. Partially close damper to raise temperature to 150°F. Place wood chips in smoker. Smoke at 150°F for 1 hour. Increase temperature to 165°F. Smoke for 5 to 6 hours longer, or until internal temperature of largest sausage registers 152°F. (Times are approximate and will vary, depending on size and diameter of sausages, weather conditions and type of smoker used.)

Remove sausages from smoker and flush sausages with cold water until internal temperature registers 120°F. Store sausages, tightly wrapped, in refrigerator for no longer than 1 week, or wrap tightly and freeze up to 2 months for best quality.

Pepper Summer Sausage

4 lbs. lean ground venison, crumbled
1 lb. pork back fat, cut into 1-inch pieces
3 oz. Fermento
3 tablespoons canning/pickling salt
2 tablespoons powdered dextrose
1 to 2 tablespoons coarsely ground pepper
1 tablespoon mustard seed

1 level teaspoon Insta Cure No. 1 (formerly Prague Powder No. 1)
1 teaspoon garlic powder
1 teaspoon onion powder
1½ to 3 cups hickory wood chips
3 to 4 synthetic-fibrous casings, 3½ to 12 inches

About 5 lbs. (2 oz. per serving)

Follow directions above.

Nutritional information not available because there is no nutritional data available for Fermento or Insta Cure No. 1.

NOTE: See page 128 for mail-order source for Fermento, powdered dextrose and Insta Cure No. 1.

Jerky

To preserve meat, Native Americans and early settlers would hang the meat over a smoky fire until it was dry. Then it could be stored or carried long distances without spoiling.

Any lean game meat without tendons or sinews can be used to make jerky. Cut meat with the grain for a chewy texture or across the grain for a more tender jerky.

Traditionally, jerky is smoked, but it can also be flavored with liquid smoke and dried in a cool oven (directions opposite) or dehydrator.

Use a curing salt like Morton® TenderQuick® mix when preparing jerky, to help prevent bacterial growth.

Cajun Jerky ↑

MARINADE:
- 4 cups cold water
- 2 to 3 tablespoons Cajun seasoning
- 2 tablespoons Morton® TenderQuick® mix
- 1 tablespoon soy sauce
- 1 to 2 teaspoons paprika

- 2 lbs. boneless venison round steak or roast, cut into 4 × 1 × ¼-inch strips
- 1½ to 3 cups hickory wood chips

11 servings (40 to 50 slices)

Follow directions on opposite page.

Nutritional information not available because there is no nutritional data available for TenderQuick mix.

How to Make Jerky

1. USE a special slicing board (see page 128 for mail-order source) and a very sharp knife to ensure even thickness of meat strips. The lip along the edges and a special insert board help guide the knife. Meat is easier to slice if it is partially frozen.

2. COMBINE marinade ingredients in large nonmetallic mixing bowl. Stir to dissolve salt cure. Add meat strips. Cover with plastic wrap. Refrigerate 24 hours, stirring occasionally. In large mixing bowl, cover wood chips with water. Soak for 1 hour. Place oven thermometer in smoker. Heat smoker to 120°F.

3. SPRAY smoker racks with nonstick vegetable cooking spray. Set aside. Drain wood chips. Drain and discard marinade from meat strips. Pat strips lightly with paper towels. Arrange strips at least ¼ inch apart on prepared racks. Place racks in smoker.

4. OPEN damper. Place a handful of wood chips in smoker. Close damper, cracking slightly when wood chips begin to smoke. Smoke meat strips for 3 to 6 hours, or until dry but not brittle, adding wood chips as necessary. Cool completely. Store jerky, loosely wrapped, in refrigerator for no longer than 1 week, or wrap tightly and freeze up to 2 months.

Oven Method for Making Jerky

1. ADD 2 teaspoons liquid smoke flavoring to marinade. Continue with recipe as directed, except place oven thermometer in oven. Heat oven to lowest possible temperature setting, propping oven door with wooden spoon so it is open about 7 inches at top to maintain 120°F.

2. SPRAY four 14 × 10-inch cooling racks with nonstick vegetable cooking spray. Arrange meat strips on prepared racks, spacing as directed. Dry for 3 to 4 hours, or until jerky is dry but not brittle.

Jerky-cured Smoked Roast

MARINADE:

- 2 cups cold water
- 1 can (12 oz.) lager-style beer
- 3 tablespoons Morton® TenderQuick® mix
- 2 tablespoons red wine vinegar
- 2 tablespoons Worcestershire sauce
- 1 tablespoon dried onion flakes
- 1 teaspoon garlic powder
- ½ teaspoon white pepper

1½ to 2-lb. venison round roast
1½ to 3 cups hickory or mesquite wood chips

8 to 12 servings

In large nonmetallic mixing bowl, combine marinade ingredients. Stir to dissolve salt cure. Add roast. Cover with plastic wrap. Refrigerate 24 hours, turning roast and stirring marinade occasionally. In large mixing bowl, cover wood chips with water. Soak for 1 hour. Place oven thermometer in smoker. Heat smoker to 130°F.

Spray smoker rack with nonstick vegetable cooking spray. Drain wood chips. Drain and discard marinade from roast. Pat roast dry with paper towels. Place roast on prepared rack. Place rack in smoker. Open damper. Maintain temperature at 130°F for 30 minutes, or until surface of roast is dry. Partially close damper to raise temperature to 150°F. Place wood chips in smoker. Smoke at 150°F for 5 to 6 hours, or until internal temperature of roast registers at least 140°F. (Times are approximate and will vary, depending on size and diameter of roast, weather conditions and type of smoker used.)

Cool roast. Store roast, tightly wrapped, in refrigerator for no longer than 1 week, or wrap tightly and freeze up to 2 months for best quality.

Nutritional information not available because there is no nutritional data available for TenderQuick mix.

Pemmican ←

Pemmican gave Native Americans and pioneers a more nutritious diet than straight jerky did. Then, it was made from powdered jerky, crushed berries and melted animal fat. Wrap individual pieces of our updated version in plastic wrap for a high-energy snack when you are on the trail.

8	oz. venison jerky
1	cup raisins
1	cup snipped dried apricots
½	cup ground walnuts
1	tablespoon grated fresh orange peel
¼	teaspoon ground allspice
⅓	cup vegetable shortening or lard, melted

40 balls

Process jerky in food processor until very finely chopped. Set aside. In same food processor, combine raisins, apricots, walnuts, peel and allspice. Process until finely ground. Return jerky to food processor. Process until mixture forms into ball and no longer sticks to side of bowl.

Roll mixture into forty 1-inch balls. Store pemmican balls between layers of wax paper in airtight container. Store in refrigerator.

Nutritional information not available due to jerky.

Ground Meat Jerky ↑

2	lbs. lean ground venison, crumbled	1½	teaspoons garlic powder
2	teaspoons canning/pickling salt	1½	teaspoons onion powder
2	teaspoons freshly ground pepper	½	teaspoon dry mustard
		1½	to 3 cups hickory wood chips

18 servings (72 strips)

In large mixing bowl, combine all ingredients, except wood chips. Mix well. Using rolling pin, roll mixture in batches between layers of wax paper to ¼-inch thickness. Remove top layer of wax paper. Cut meat into 3 × 1-inch strips. Using spatula, transfer strips to cooling racks that have been sprayed with nonstick vegetable cooking spray, spacing at least ½ inch apart.

Smoke jerky as directed on page 115.

Variation: To prepare jerky in oven, add 1 to 2 teaspoons liquid smoke to meat mixture. Follow directions on page 115.

Per Serving: Calories: 134 • Protein: 10 g. • Carbohydrate: <1 g. • Fat: 10 g.
• Cholesterol: 45 mg. • Sodium: 185 mg.
Exchanges: 1½ medium-fat meat, ½ fat

Deer Camp Recipes

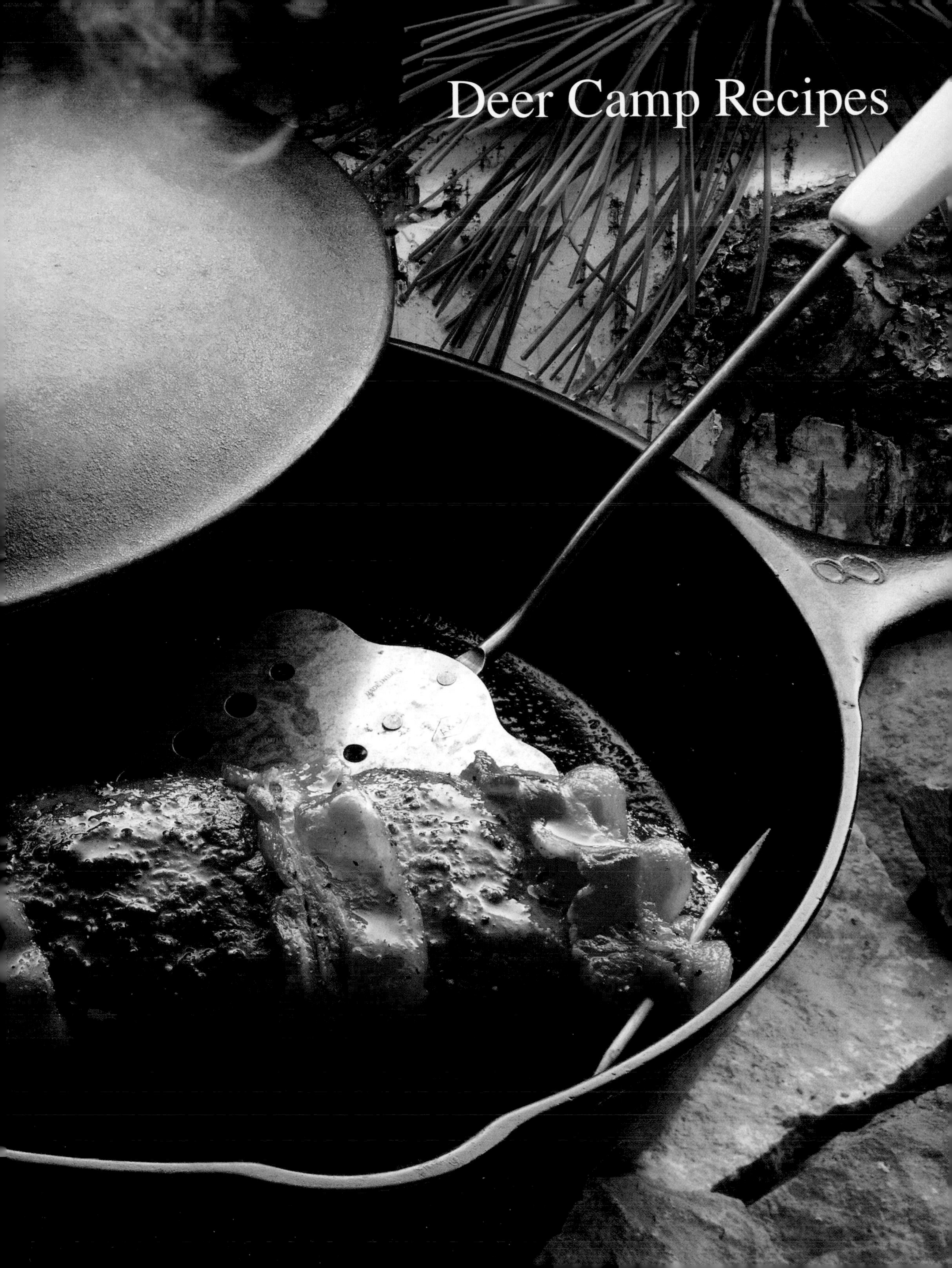

Deer Camp Recipes

Enjoying the bounty of a good day's hunt is one of the greatest pleasures of deer hunting. After a freshly taken deer is field-dressed, there are some choice cuts that can be enjoyed right away as a reward for work well done.

The best cut of all is, of course, the tenderloin. This is the one cut that often doesn't make it home, since it is easy to remove from the cavity of a field-dressed deer and seems to taste best from a freshly taken deer. Oftentimes, the best way to prepare it is to simply panfry it in a little butter with nothing more than salt and pepper to season it. We've included some new tenderloin recipes that are easy to prepare and won't overwhelm this excellent cut.

Other cuts that are at their best when fresh are the heart and liver. In the following pages, you will find an easy technique for cutting up the heart, along with three simple, but flavorful, recipes. We've also included a version of the most popular liver recipe – Liver & Onions.

These deer camp recipes will provide you with delicious new ways to enjoy fresh venison at camp using simple ingredients that are easy to pack. The recipes can be made over a camp stove, campfire or grill. We've also kept the preparation simple, so you won't have to wait long to enjoy your dinner.

Spiced Grilled Tenderloin ●VERY FAST LOW-FAT →

Make the spice mix ahead of time and keep it in a small jar with your camping gear.

SPICE MIX:
1½ teaspoons pepper
1½ teaspoons ground allspice
 1 teaspoon salt
 ¾ teaspoon ground cinnamon
 ¾ teaspoon ground cloves
 ½ teaspoon ground nutmeg

 1 tablespoon vegetable oil or olive oil
   Venison tenderloin (about 1 lb.)

3 to 4 servings

In small bowl, combine spice mix ingredients. Add oil and mix well to make a paste. Rub all sides of tenderloin evenly with spice paste. Set aside.

Prepare grill or campfire for medium direct heat. Place tenderloin on cooking grid. Grill for 12 to 14 minutes, or until meat is desired doneness, turning tenderloin occasionally. Let stand for 5 minutes before slicing.

Per Serving: Calories: 173 • Protein: 26 g. • Carbohydrate: 2 g. • Fat: 6 g. • Cholesterol: 95 mg. • Sodium: 598 mg.
Exchanges: 3 very lean meat, 1¼ fat

Bacon-wrapped Tenderloin ●VERY FAST

¼ teaspoon salt
¼ teaspoon onion powder
¼ teaspoon garlic powder
¼ teaspoon pepper
   Venison tenderloin (about 1 lb.)
 2 strips bacon
 1 tablespoon butter or margarine

3 to 4 servings

In small bowl, combine salt, onion powder, garlic powder and pepper. Rub all sides of tenderloin evenly with spice mixture. Wrap bacon strips in a spiral around tenderloin, securing ends with wooden picks.

Heat 10-inch cast-iron skillet over medium heat. Melt butter in skillet. Add tenderloin. Cook for 4 to 6 minutes, or until meat is browned on all sides. Reduce heat to low or set skillet off direct heat. Cover. Cook for 12 to 15 minutes, or until meat is desired doneness, turning tenderloin occasionally. Let stand for 5 minutes before slicing.

Per Serving: Calories: 226 • Protein: 27 g. • Carbohydrate: <1 g. • Fat: 12 g. • Cholesterol: 112 mg. • Sodium: 300 mg.
Exchanges: 3¼ very lean meat, 2½ fat

Korean Venison Barbecue

Mix up the marinade for this flavorful dish at home, then take it to deer camp in a small, tightly sealed jar or container.

MARINADE:

⅓ cup soy sauce

3 tablespoons sugar

2 tablespoons sesame oil

2 teaspoons dehydrated minced onions

½ teaspoon ground ginger

¼ teaspoon garlic powder

Freshly ground pepper to taste

Venison tenderloin (about 1 lb.), cut into ¼-inch slices

3 to 4 servings

In shallow dish, combine marinade ingredients. Add tenderloin slices, stirring to coat. Let stand for 15 minutes, stirring occasionally.

Heat 10-inch cast-iron skillet over medium-high heat. Using slotted spoon, transfer tenderloin to skillet. Cook for 3 to 4 minutes, or until meat is no longer pink, stirring frequently. Serve tenderloin slices on bread or buns, or over a baked potato, if desired.

Per Serving: Calories: 191 • Protein: 26 g. • Carbohydrate: 6 g. • Fat: 6 g. • Cholesterol: 95 mg. • Sodium: 746 mg.
Exchanges: 3 very lean meat, 1¼ fat

Blackened Tenderloin

This Cajun treatment of venison tenderloin is a natural for outdoor cooking with a cast-iron skillet. Make the seasoning mix before you leave home.

SEASONING MIX:

2 teaspoons chili powder

1 teaspoon ground cumin

½ teaspoon black pepper

½ teaspoon chili powder

¼ teaspoon white pepper

Venison tenderloin (about 1 lb.), cut into ½-inch slices

2 tablespoons vegetable oil

3 to 4 servings

In shallow dish or plate, combine seasoning mix ingredients. Pound or press tenderloin slices to ¼-inch thickness. Dredge slices in seasoning mix to coat.

In 10-inch cast-iron skillet, heat oil over medium-high heat. Add tenderloin slices. Cook for 3 to 4 minutes, or until meat is well browned, turning slices over once.

Per Serving: Calories: 203 • Protein: 26 g. • Carbohydrate: 1 g. • Fat: 10 g. • Cholesterol: 95 mg. • Sodium: 63 mg.
Exchanges: 3 very lean meat, 2 fat

Liver & Onions

⬤ VERY FAST

⅓ cup all-purpose flour
½ teaspoon salt
¼ teaspoon pepper
1 lb. venison liver, cut into
   ½-inch slices
4 slices bacon, cut into 1-inch
   pieces
2 medium onions, sliced

4 servings

In shallow dish or on sheet of wax paper, combine flour, salt and pepper. Dredge liver slices in flour mixture to coat. Set aside.

In 10-inch cast-iron skillet, cook bacon over medium heat for 4 to 5 minutes, or until bacon is crisp, turning occasionally. Remove bacon from skillet and drain on paper towels.

Add liver and onions to bacon drippings in skillet. Cook for 6 to 8 minutes, or until meat is well done, stirring occasionally. Top liver and onions with bacon pieces.

Nutritional information not available.

Stuffed Venison Heart Rolls ⬤ VERY FAST

Mix up the stuffing ingredients ahead of time, and carry them to camp in a small, sealable plastic bag.

1 venison heart (8 oz.), sliced as
　　directed at right

STUFFING:
½ cup unseasoned dry bread
　　crumbs
1 teaspoon dried parsley flakes
¼ teaspoon dried thyme leaves
¼ teaspoon rubbed sage
¼ teaspoon seasoned salt

3 tablespoons water
　Pepper to taste
4 strips bacon
2 tablespoons butter or margarine

2 servings

How to Slice Heart for Stuffed Venison Heart Rolls

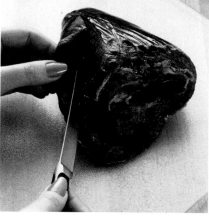

SLIP knife lengthwise into outer wall of heart, penetrating only half the thickness of the wall.

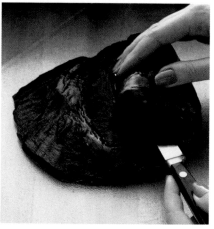

SLICE in spiral fashion, from outside to center, "unrolling" heart into one long strip. Remove and discard membranes. Continue with directions below.

In small mixing bowl, combine stuffing ingredients and water. Stir until evenly moistened. Spoon and pack stuffing mixture on cut side of heart. Roll up heart, enclosing stuffing. Sprinkle heart with pepper to taste.

Wrap bacon strips around heart, securing with wooden picks. Cut heart between picks into 4 rolls.

Heat 10-inch cast-iron skillet over medium heat. Melt butter in skillet. Add rolls. Cook for 8 to 10 minutes, or until meat is desired doneness, turning rolls over once or twice.

Nutritional information not available.

124

Heart with Horseradish Sauce

HORSERADISH SAUCE:

⅓ cup mayonnaise
2 tablespoons prepared horseradish, well drained
1 teaspoon sugar
¼ teaspoon Worcestershire sauce

2 tablespoons all-purpose flour
½ teaspoon paprika
¼ teaspoon seasoned salt
1 venison heart (8 oz.), cut crosswise into ¼-inch slices
2 tablespoons vegetable oil

2 servings

In small mixing bowl, combine all sauce ingredients. Set aside. In shallow dish or on sheet of wax paper, combine flour, paprika and salt. Dredge heart slices in flour mixture to coat.

In 10-inch cast-iron skillet, heat oil over medium heat. Add heart slices. Cook for 4 to 6 minutes, or until meat is desired doneness. Serve with horseradish sauce.

TIP: Prepare horseradish sauce and flour mixture ahead of time.

Nutritional information not available.

Panfried Heart Strips

1 venison heart (8 oz.)
   Pepper to taste
½ to 1 teaspoon salt
1 to 2 tablespoons butter or margarine, cut in pieces
1 teaspoon Worcestershire sauce

2 servings

Cut and unroll heart into 1 long strip (see technique in Stuffed Venison Heart Rolls, opposite). Cut long strip into 3 × 2-inch strips. Pat dry with paper towel. Sprinkle strips with pepper to taste.

Sprinkle salt in even layer in 10-inch cast-iron skillet. Heat skillet over medium-high heat. When salt begins to brown, lay strips flat in skillet. Sear strips for 10 seconds per side. Add butter to skillet. Cook for 2 to 3 minutes, or until meat is desired doneness. Sprinkle with Worcestershire sauce just before serving.

TIP: Squeeze a fresh lemon over panfried strips just before serving to add tang and cut the richness of the dish.

Nutritional information not available.

Index

Cowles Creative Publishing, Inc. offers a variety
of how-to books. For information write:

Cowles Creative Publishing
Subscriber Books
5900 Green Oak Drive
Minnetonka, MN 55343

Sources for sausage and smoking equipment and supplies include:

Cumberland General Store,
Route 3, Crossville TN 38555;
800-334-4640

*(Smokers, smokehouses, grinders, stuffers;
synthetic-fibrous casings, Morton® salt
cures, Insta Cure [Prague Powder], soy
protein concentrate and seasoning blends)*

Hi Mountain Jerky,
1000 College View Road, Riverton WY 82501;
800-829-2285

*(Slicing board, jerky drying screens; pre-
mixed sausage and jerky seasoning blends)*

The Sausage Maker,
26 Military Road, Buffalo NY 14207;
716-876-5521

*(Smokers, grinders, stuffers; casings;
smoking sawdust; specialty sausage supplies
including Insta Cure [Prague Powder] and
Fermento, soy protein concentrate; premixed
sausage and jerky seasoning blends)*